Aldous Huxley was born in 1894, the third son of Leonard Huxley (the biographer and editor of *Cornhill Magazine*) and the grandson of Thomas Henry Huxley. His mother, who died when Aldous was fourteen, was the niece of Matthew Arnold; Sir Julian Huxley was his brother.

In 1916 Aldous Huxley took a first in English at Balliol College, Oxford, despite a condition of near-blindness which had developed while he was at Eton. During 1919 he married Maria Nys, a Belgian, and in the same year he joined *The Athenaeum* under Middleton Murry, Katherine Mansfield's husband. His first book of verse had been published in 1916 and two more followed. Then, in 1920, *Limbo*, a collection of short stories, was published. A year later *Crome Yellow*, Huxley's first novel, appeared and his reputation was firmly established. From the first, the public recognized that the strength of Huxley's writing lay in his combination of dazzling dialogue and surface cynicism (often very funny indeed) with a foundation of great conviction in the emancipating influences he was to exert.

For most of the 1920s Huxley lived in Italy but in the 30s moved to Sanary, near Toulon, where he wrote *Brave New World*. During this decade he was deeply concerned with the Peace Pledge Union but left Europe in 1937 as he believed the Californian climate would help his eyesight, a constant burden. It was in California that he became convinced of the value of mystical experience and he described the effects of some of his experiments in *Doors of Perception* and *Heaven and Hell*.

Maria Nys Huxley died in 1955 and a year later Aldous married Laura Archera, a concert violinist who had become a practising psycho-therapist. They continued to live in California where Aldous Huxley died, in 1963.

ALDOUS HUXLEY

Jesting Pilate

The Diary of a Journey

TRIAD
PALADIN

Triad/Paladin Books
Granada Publishing Ltd
8 Grafton Street, London W1X 3LA

Published by Triad/Paladin Books 1985

Triad Paperbacks Ltd is an imprint of
Chatto, Bodley Head & Jonathan Cape Ltd and
Granada Publishing Ltd

First published in Great Britain by
Chatto & Windus Ltd 1926
Copyright © Mrs Laura Huxley 1926

ISBN 0-586-08511-4

Printed and bound in Great Britain by
Collins, Glasgow

Set in Baskerville

Contents

PART ONE
India & Burma

Port Said

The after-hatch was off. Hung high above the opening, the electric lights glared down into the deep square well of the hold. The watcher, leaning over the brink of the well, shouted and waved his arms. The donkey-engine rattled responsively. Twenty sacks of potatoes came rushing up from the depths. Ten feet above the level of the deck, they were swung sideways by the transverse pull of a second rope, hung suspended for a moment beyond the gunwale, then, at another signal from the watcher, dropped down into the waiting lighter. The watcher raised his hand again; again the engine rattled. Two empty loops of rope came up over the ship's side, whipped across the deck and went down, writhing like living snakes, into the well. At the bottom, far down, little men caught at the trailing ropes, piled up the sacks, made fast. The watcher shouted. Yet another quintal of potatoes came rushing up, swung sideways, dropped out of sight over the edge of the ship. And so it continued, all the night. Curiously, admiringly, and at last with a growing sense of horror, I looked on. Moving bits of matter from one point of the world's surface to another – man's whole activity. And the wisdom of the East, I reflected, consists in the affirmation that it is better to leave the bits of matter where they are. Up to a point, no doubt, the sages of the East are right. There are many bits of matter which might be left in their place and nobody would be any the worse. These particles of ink, for example, which I so laboriously transfer from their bottle to the surface of the paper . . .

We landed – in what a sink! At Port Said they speak all languages, accept every currency. But their exchange is robbery and they employ their gift of tongues only for cheating. The staple industry of the place seems to be the manufacture and sale of indecent photographs. They are stocked in almost every shop; they are pressed upon you – at prices that decline astonishingly, as you walk away, from a sovereign to half a crown – by every loafer. The copiousness of the supply is proof of a correspondingly large demand for these wares by passing travellers. In these matters, it seems, many people are more agreeably excited by the representation – whether pictorial or verbal – than by carnal reality. It is a curious psychological fact, for which I can find no complete explanation.

In the Red Sea

Talking with Europeans who live and work in the East, I find that, if they love the East (which they mostly do), it is always for the same reason. In the East, they say, a man is somebody; he has authority and is looked up to; he knows all the people who matter and is known. At home, he is lost in the crowd, he does not count, he is nobody. Life in the East satisfies the profoundest and most powerful of all the instincts – that of self-assertion. The young man who goes out from a London suburb to take up a clerkship in India finds himself a member of a small ruling community; he has slavish servants to order about, dark-skinned subordinates to whom it is right and proper to be rude. Three hundred and twenty million Indians surround him; he feels incomparably superior to them all, from the coolie to the maharaja, from the untouchable to the thoroughbred Brahmin, from the illiterate peasant to the holder of half a dozen European degrees. He may be ill-bred, stupid, uneducated; no matter. His skin is white. Superiority in India is a question of epiderms. No wonder if he loves the East. For the European, Eastern conditions of life are a kind of intoxicant. But the tipsiness they produce is more satisfactory than that which results from the absorption of whisky. Alcohol, as the anonymous poet has said:

> Bids valour burgeon in strong men,
> Quickens the poet's wit and pen,
> Despises fate.

But the sense of power which it gives, the feeling of grandeur and importance, are purely illusory and do not last. The intoxication of the East is permanent, and the sense of greatness is not entirely an illusion. The commercial traveller who goes East is really a greater man (so long as he remains in the East) than his colleague in patent medicines at home. Sobriety supervenes only when he returns to Europe. In the West he finds his natural place in the social hierarchy. One out of London's suburban millions, he feels homesick for the East. It is not to be wondered at. What man likes to be sediment, when he might float gallantly on the sunlit surface?

At Sea

Everybody in the ship menaces us with the prospect of a very 'good time' in India. A good time means going to the races, playing bridge, drinking cocktails, dancing till four in the morning, and talking about nothing. And meanwhile the beautiful, the incredible world in which we live awaits our exploration, and life is short, and time flows stanchlessly, like blood from a mortal wound. And there is all knowledge, all art. There are men and women, the innumerable living, and, in books, the souls of those dead who deserved to be immortal. Heaven preserve me, in such a world, from having a Good Time! Heaven helps those who help themselves. I shall see to it that my time in India is as bad as I can make it.

Bombay

On the quay, awaiting the disembarkment of their relatives on board our ship, stand four or five Parsi ladies – all ugly, as only members of that exclusive, inbred race can be ugly. They wear Indian *saris*, with European blouses, stockings, and high-heeled canvas shoes. In one hand they hold black umbrellas, in the other garlands of flowers. The black umbrellas are for use against the sun; the wreaths of tuberoses and oleanders are to hang round the necks of their returning friends. One of the ladies, we are confidentially informed, is an eminent woman doctor.

A dozen coolies, thin-limbed like spider-monkeys, are drafted to wheel up the gangway. They lay their hands on it, they simultaneously utter a loud cry – in the hope, evidently, that the gangway will take fright and move of its own accord. But their faith is insufficient; the gangway does not stir. Sadly, with sighs, they make up their mind to shove. A vulgar, commonplace, and tiring method of making things move. But at least it works. The gangway rolls across the quay, is hoisted into position. Passengers begin to leave the ship. The friends and relations of the Parsi ladies at last come down the plank. They are embraced, lassoed with flowers, and led off to the attendant Hupmobiles and Overlands behind the Custom House. It is our first view of the East.

The brown skins, the bare feet, the nose-rings, the humped bullocks – all these things were foreseeable, seemed obvious and familiar from the moment of landing. The really odd, unexpected thing about Bombay was its birds. There are more birds in the streets of this million-peopled city than in an English woodland. Huge kites, their wings spread and unmoving, go soaring along the thoroughfares, effortlessly keeping pace with the traffic below. Innumerable grey-headed crows fly hither and thither, sit perched on every roof, every sill and wire. Their cawing is the fundmental bass to every other sound in Bombay. Kites and crows do useful scavenging work, and Bombay, which produces much garbage and few dustmen, keeps them well employed and copiously fed. Nobody, in this land where the killing of animals is all but murder, does them or their nests any harm. They increase and multiply, they are astonishingly unafraid. All over India we were to find the same abundance of bird life, the same trustful absence of fear. Coming from Italy, where, for nine months of the year, while *lo sport* is in progress, the countryside is almost birdless, where armed men lie ambushed half a day for a hedge-sparrow, and migrant warblers are netted and eaten by the thousand – coming from Italy, I was particularly impressed by the number and variety of Indian birds.

Bombay

Architecturally, Bombay is one of the most appalling cities of either hemisphere. It had the misfortune to develop during what was, perhaps, the darkest period of all architectural history. Most of its public buildings were designed and executed between 1860 and 1900. It is hardly necessary for me to expatiate or comment. All that need be said has been said perfectly in the guide-book; then, let the guide-book speak. The Presidential Secretariat, we are told, is in 'the Venetian Gothic style.' The University Hall (completed 1874), which is 'in the French Decorated style of the fifteenth century,' rubs shoulders with the 'Early English' Law Courts (opened in 1879). The University Library, harking back to an earlier century than the Hall, is 'in the style of fourteenth century Gothic.' The Old General Post Office 'was designed in the medieval style by Mr Trubshawe.' (Mr Trubshawe was cautiously unspecific.) The Telegraph Office (date not mentioned, but my knowledge of architectural fashions makes me inclined to a rather later epoch) is 'Romanesque.' The Victoria Station, of which the style is 'Italian Gothic with certain oriental modifications in the domes,' confronts the Municipal Buildings, in which 'the oriental feeling introduced into the Gothic architecture has a pleasing effect.' More frankly oriental are the Gateway of India ('based on the work of the sixteenth century in Gujarat') and the Prince of Wales Museum ('based on the Indian work of the fifteenth and sixteenth centuries in the Presidency.') The architecture of the Hotel Majestic and the Taj Mahal Hotel is not described in the guide-book. It is a remissness; they deserve description. The Majestic is more wildly Mohammedan than anything that the most orthodox of Great Moguls ever dreamed of, and the gigantic Taj combines the style of the South Kensington Natural History Museum with that of an Indian pavilion at an International Exhibition. After an hour passed among these treasures of modern architecture, I took a cab, and in mere self-defence drove to the Town Hall, which is a quiet, late-Georgian affair, built in the 'thirties. Long and low, with its flight of steps, its central pediment, its Doric colonnade, it has an air of calm and quiet decency. Among so many architectural cads and pretentious bounders, it is almost the only gentleman. In Bombay, it seems as good as the Parthenon.

Bombay

In the lounge of the hotel is a bookstall, stocked with periodicals and novels – my own, I was gratified to see, among them. One whole section of the bookstall is devoted to the sale of English and American technical journals – but technical journals of a single, rather special kind. Journals of gynaecology, of obstetrics, of sexual psychology, of venereal disease. Rows of them, and dozens of copies of each. The hotel lounge is not specially frequented by doctors; it is the general public which buys these journals. Strange, strange phenomenon! Perhaps it is one of the effects of the climate.

Bombay

From its island body, Bombay radiates long tentacles of suburban squalor into the land. Mills and huge grey tenements, low huts among the palm-trees flank the outgoing roads for miles, and the roads themselves are thronged with the coming and going of innumerable passengers. Driving out of Bombay along one of these populous highways, I felt (but more acutely) that amazement which often overwhelms me when I pass through the sordid fringes of some European city – amazement at my own safety and comfort, at the security of my privileges, at the unthinking and almost unresentful acceptance of millions of my less fortunate fellow-beings of my claim to be educated, leisured, comparatively wealthy. That I and my privileged fellows should be tolerated by our own people seems to me strange enough. But that our pretensions, which are still higher in India than in Europe, should be allowed by these innumerable dark-skinned strangers, over whom we rule, strikes me as being still more extraordinary.

We are accepted much as paper money is accepted, because there is a general belief that we are worth something. Our value is not intrinsic, but borrowed from the opinion of the world. We live and rule on credit and are respected, not so much because we are really formidable (though our power is great) as because there exists a convention that we should be respected. The less fortunate majority is carefully educated in this useful opinion. Our paper currency has begun to lose its conventional value in Europe. We still continue to offer ourselves (often with a certain secret diffidence) as five-pound notes; but the more sceptical of our 'inferiors' refuse to regard us as anything more precious than waste paper. When the same thing begins to happen in India, when the credit on which the white man has been living and ruling for so long is withdrawn, what then? Without any violence, merely by quietly refusing to accept the white man at his own valuation, merely by declining to have anything to do with him, the Indian can reduce British rule to impotence. Non- co-operation has failed, up till now, owing to inefficiency of organization and a lack of public spirit on the part of the Indians. But efficient organization and public spirit are the products of a special education. When the masses have received that education, when the paper money of European prestige has been systematically discredited and individual Europeans are boycotted and left suspended in a kind of social and economic vacuum, the Indians will be able to get whatever they ask for. (The mere disappearance of all Indian servants would be almost enough in itself to bring the white man to terms. Faced with the prospect of having to empty his own slops, a Viceroy would begin to listen with an increased sympathy to Swarajist demands.) Whether the Indians will succeed any better than the English in the task of governing India, is another question. Swaraj may prove a blessing, or it may turn out to be a catastrophe. But in any case it will be obtained whenever a sufficient number of India's three hundred and twenty millions make up their minds systematically to ask for it; the thing is obvious. They have only to be incredulous of the white man's pretensions, they have only to ignore his almost invisible presence among their multitudes; that is all.

In the meantime, however, our credit holds, at any rate among the masses. The educated Indian may doubt whether our five-pound notes are worth more than an equal area snipped out of the *Daily Mail*; but his uneducated brother still accepts us at our face value. Thin-legged pedestrians salute me as I pass. Through the squalor of suburban Bombay, I carry my privileges of comfort, culture, and wealth in perfect safety. They are still secure, more or less, even in the suburbs of an English manufacturing town. For how long? Rolling along between the palm-trees, I wonder.

Bombay

It has been our good fortune, while in Bombay, to meet Mrs Sarojini Naidu, the newly-elected President of the All-India Congress and a woman who combines in the most remarkable way great intellectual power with charm, sweetness and courageous energy, a wide culture with originality, and earnestness with humour. If all Indian politicians are like Mrs Naidu, then the country is fortunate indeed.

At a tea-party in her rooms, a young Mohammedan of Arab descent recited some verses in Urdu by the modern Panjabi poet Iqbal. The subject was Sicily (and 'Sicily,' alas, was the only word in the poem which I could understand). The poet, we were told, had been inspired to write while passing through the Straits of Messina on his return from a European voyage, and his poem was in the nature of a lament – a Mohammedan's indignant lament that the island which had once belonged to the Musulmans should now be in the hands of infidels. I did not say so at the time, but I must confess that the idea of Sicily as a Mohammedan country cruelly ravished from its rightful owners, the Arabs, struck me as rather shocking. For us good Europeans, Sicily is Greek, is Latin, is Christian, is Italian. The Arab occupation is an interlude, an irrelevance. True, the Arabs in Sicily were the best sort of civilized Arabs. But it is hard for us to regard them as anything but trespassers on that classical ground. And now I was being expected to look upon Theocritus's island – just as Italians before the War looked on the Trentino and other fragments of *Italia irredenta* – as a piece of 'unredeemed Araby.' It was asking too much. For the first moment, I felt quite indignant – just as indignant, no doubt, as the poet had felt at the sight of those once Mohammedan shores now polluted by Christians. In the traveller's life these little lessons in the theory of relativity are daily events.

The words of the poem were incomprehensible to me. But at least I was able to appreciate the way in which it was recited, or rather chanted – for the stanzas were set to a regularly recurrent melody in the minor key. Each verse began with a stirring phrase that rose, like the call of a trumpet, from the dominant to the tonic, and, at the next strong beat, to the minor third. After that, the melody mournfully wandered; there were suspended notes and long shakes on a single vowel. It was thus, I felt sure, as I listened, it was thus that the Greek choruses must have been recited – to a chant kept well within the limits of a single octave, a chant (to our ears, at least) somewhat monotonous, sung without strain, more in a speaking voice than in what we should regard as a singing voice. And in the suspended notes, in the shakes and warblings over a single long-drawn syllable, I seemed to recognize that distinguishing feature of the Euripidean chorus which Aristophanes derides and parodies in the *Frogs*.

Bombay

This evening a congratulatory address was presented to Mr Patel, the new Speaker of the Legislative Assembly, by the members of his community, an agricultural sub-caste of Gujarat. Other members of the community have broken through the traditionary trammels – the hall was full of men who had left the ancestral plough for work in the city – but none has previously risen to a position so exalted as that attained by Mr Patel. 'From Ploughboy to President' – Indian journalists, like their colleagues across the sea, have a weakness for phrases – was the phrase in which the newspapers summed up Mr Patel's career.

We accompanied Mrs Naidu to the function and, as her guests, found ourselves sitting in places of honour on the platform. The hall was crowded. The heat, though the sun had set, was prodigious. (It is one of the peculiarities of the Bombay climate that the temperature rises, or at any rate seems to rise, during the first hours of the night.) In the garden outside, a band was playing the fox-trots of two or three seasons ago.

The programme of the function had been carefully worked out. A chorus of children was to sing during the period of waiting before Mr Patel entered. Somebody was to recite a congratulatory poem when he had taken his seat. Then there were to be speeches, with Mr Patel's reply and the presentation of the address in its silver casket to finish off the proceedings. A perfect programme, on paper; but in practice, as it turned out, not quite so good as it might have been. For the band played and the audience talked all through the children's singing; indeed, it was only quite by chance, because I happened to notice that they were opening and shutting their mouths in an unnatural, fish-like sort of way, that I came to know that the children were singing at all. And when the reciter began intoning his congratulatory poem, the indefatigable band struck up the tune of 'Why did you kiss that Girl?' – the poem was lost. But by this time some few thousands of Bombay's innumerable population of crows had settled in the trees outside the hall and were discussing the question, as gregarious birds will do at sunset, of retiring for the night. Their cawing was portentous. Never in Europe have I heard anything like it. I was sitting on the platform, within a few feet of the speakers; but their voices were quite inaudible, even to me. It was only some half an hour later, when the crows had dropped off to sleep, that any word can have reached the audience. After that the proceedings went off pretty smoothly and with only a little hitch or two about the reading of the address and the presentation of the casket to mar the solemnity of the occasion.

I was reminded very much of analogous functions in Italy. There is no word of which Italian journalists are fonder than the word *solenne*. Every ceremony of which you read an account in an Italian newspaper is solemn – solemn foundation-stone layings, solemn depositings of wreaths on tombs, solemn celebrations of centenaries, solemn royal entrances and exits. In the papers, as I say, all these things are solemn. In practice, however, they are rarely anything but slipshod, haphazard, and to northern eyes at any rate, ineffective and unimpressive. The good Catholic who comes to Rome in the hope of seeing noble and soul-stirring religious ceremonies, generally returns disappointed to his own country. The fact is that they order these things better in France, in England, in Belgium, in Germany – in any northern land. We Northerners stage-manage our effects more professionally than do the people of the south. We take pains to impress ourselves; and at the same time we give the ceremony which we have staged every chance of seeming impressive to us by deliberately throwing ourselves into a serious state of mind and consistently keeping our seriousness till the function is over. The Southerner declines to take trouble over the details of stage-management, and will not be bothered to hold one mental attitude for a long time at a stretch. To us, in consequence, he seems disgracefully slipshod, cynical, and irreverent.

But we must not be over-hasty in our judgments. The Southerner has his own traditions about these matters, and they happen to be different from ours. In this respect, I should guess, his habits of thought and feeling are nearer to the Oriental's than to ours. Let us try to understand before we condemn.

We call the Southerner slipshod because he tolerates shabbiness among his grandeurs, and permits his solemnities to be marred by a ludicrous inefficiency. But he could retort by calling us crassly unimaginative because we are incapable of seeing the fine intention through the inadequate medium of its expression, of appreciating the noble general effect in spite of the shabbiness of the details. For in matters of art, he would argue (and a religious ceremony, a civic or political function are forms of art, being only solemn ballets and symbolical charades), it is the intention and the general effect that count. Those little struts and flying buttresses of marble, with which the Greeks strengthened their statues, are absurd, if you choose to consider them closely. But they are meant to be ignored. Structurally, a sham façade is ludicrous; the Southerner knows it, of course, just as well as Mr Ruskin. But, more wise than Ruskin, he does not fly into a passion of moral indignation over the falsehood of it; he permits himself to enjoy the genuine grandiosity of its appearance when seen from the right angle. In church, the priest may gabble, as though he were trying to break a world's record, the acolytes may pick their noses, the choir-boys sing out of tune, the vergers spit; we Northerners are revolted, but the wisely indulgent Southerner passes over these trivial details, and enjoys the fine general effect of the ecclesiastical ballet in spite of its little blemishes. But if he enjoys it, the Northerner now asks, why doesn't he at least sit still and refrain from laughing chatter, why doesn't he try to look, and looking, make himself feel, consistently serious? To which the other will retort by deriding the Northerner's slowness and inelasticity of mind, his pomposity, his incapacity for frankly feeling two emotions at once, or at any rate in very rapid succession. 'I can see ludicrous and shabby details just as clearly as you do,' he will say, 'and, like you, I deplore them. But I keep my sense of proportion, and do not permit mere details to interfere with my appreciation of the general effect. You have a talent for high seriousness; but I can smile and feel solemn within the same minute. In church I pray fervently at one moment, I am transported by the beauty of the ceremonial (in spite of the shoddy details), and the next I make eyes at the young woman across the aisle and talk to my neighbour about the price of rubber shares. Operatic airs, I know, are stagey and conventional, and I deride the ludicrously strutting tenor who sings them; but at the same time I rapturously applaud his bawling and abandon myself, even while I mock, to the throaty passion of the music. Your mind is clumsier, more stiffly starched than mine. You can only be one thing at a time, and you regard as shocking the nimble emotional antics of those more fortunately endowed than yourself or more reasonably brought up. For my part I can only pity you for your limitations.'

The speeches, all but that of Mrs Naidu, who gave us English eloquence, were in Gujarati, and for me, therefore, no better than gibberish. I amused myself by listening for the occasional English words with which the incomprehensibility was powered. 'Gibber gibber gibber Bombay Presidency'; it was thus that I should have reported a typical speech of the evening. 'Gibber gibber committee, gibber gibber gibber minority report, gibber gibber Government of India, gibber gibber gibber George Washington, gibber Edmund Burke, gibber gibber gibber Currency Commission, gibber gibber gibber gibber . . .' It was thus, I reflected, that our Saxon fathers borrowed from the invaders' speech the words for which they would find no equivalent in their own debased, post-Conquest English. Listening to the incomprehensible chatter of his foreign vassals, the Norman baron would have been amused to catch, every now and then, the sound of such familiar words as 'army,' 'castle,' 'law.'

The function came to an end. Festooned with flowers – for there had been a generous distribution of garlands, by which even we, albeit, quite undeserving, had profited – we followed our hostess into the garden. There under palm-trees, we drank a kind of richly perfumed soda-water, we ate strange dumplings stuffed with mincemeat that was at once sweet and violently peppery – chopped mutton mixed with a vitriolic jam – and tried to take the burning taste of them away with little cakes and sandwiches, slabs of almond icing and fried savouries. At the other side of the garden, safely removed from possible contamination, the orthodox refreshed themselves with special foods prepared by cooks of guaranteed good family. White-bearded and most majestically robed, Mr Patel moved among the guests, looking like a minor, even a major, prophet – but a prophet, as we saw when he sat down at table, with a most reassuringly humorous twinkle in his eyes.

It was nearly nine when we got back to the hotel. Coming up from dinner, an hour later, we found our room magically perfumed by the tuberoses and champaks of our garlands. That night, and all next day, till they were quite withered, the flowers poured out their scent, and the wind driven down on us by the electric fan in the ceiling was a warm air impregnated with strange and tropical sweetness.

Kashmir

It is cheaper in this country to have a waggon pulled by half a dozen men than by a pair of oxen or horses. All day, on the road below our house, the heavy-laden carts go creaking slowly along behind their team of human draft animals. The coolies sing as they pull, partly out of sheer lightness of heart (for these Kashmiris are wonderfully cheerful, in spite of everything), and partly, no doubt, because they have discovered the psychological fact that to sing in chorus creates a strengthening sense of solidarity within the singing group, and seems to lighten the work in hand by making the muscular effort respond almost automatically to a regular rhythmic stimulus. I noticed two main types of labourer's chantey. One of these is melodically quite ambitious; for it ranges over no less than three notes of the minor scale. It is sung in unison, and there is no separate chorus leader. The commonest form of the melody is more or less as follows:

Da capo ad infinitum. They sing it all day at their work and half the night as well, for fun, when there happens to be a wedding or some similar festival. The other chantey takes the form of a kind of dialogue between the chorus and a chorus leader, who responds to the two strong beats of the choral song by a single monosyllable, always the same, sustained for two beats, and sung emphatically on a lower note. The words were incomprehensible to me; but translated into terms of gibberish, they sounded something like this: *Chorus*, Dum-dum. *Leader*, Bong. *Chorus*, Tweedle-dum. *Leader*, Bong; Tum-diddy, Bong; Tweedle-weedle, Bong. And so on, hour after hour.

This rhythmical dialogue is the favourite music of the waggon teams. Walking abroad, one is never for long out of hearing of that monotonous Dum-dum, Bong; diddy-dum, Bong. The singing floats down between the poplar trees of the straight flat roads of the valley, and slowly, laboriously the waggon and its human crew come following after the swift-travelling song. Passing, I feel almost ashamed to look at the creeping wain; I avert my eyes from a spectacle so painfully accusatory. That men should be reduced to the performance of a labour which, even for beasts, is cruel and humiliating, is a dreadful thing. 'Ah, but they feel things less than we do,' the owners of motor-cars, the eaters of five meals a day, the absorbers of whisky hasten to assure me; 'they feel them less, because they're used to this sort of life. They don't mind, because they know no better. They're really quite happy.'

And these assertions are quite true. They do not know better; they *are* used to this life; they are incredibly resigned. All the more shame to the men and to the system that have reduced them to such an existence and kept them from knowing anything better.

It is in relation to their opposites that things have significance for us. 'Opposite shows up opposite, as a Frank a negro.' So wrote

Jalalu 'd-Din Muhammad Rumi. 'The opposite of light shows what
is light . . . God created grief and pain for this purpose: to wit, to
manifest happiness by its opposites. Hidden things are manifested
by their opposites; but as God has no opposite, He remains hidden.'
These Kashmiri draft coolies, who are unaware of comfort, culture,
plenty, privacy, leisure, security, freedom, do not in consequence
know that they are slaves, do not repine at being herded together in
filthy hovels like beasts, do not suffer from their ignorance, and are
resigned to being overworked and underfed. Those who profit by the
Kashmiris' ignorant acquiescence in such sub-human conditions are
naturally not anxious that they should be made aware of the
desirable opposites which would make their present life seem odious.
The spread of education, the improvement of living conditions are
causes which do not rouse them to enthusiasm. And yet, in spite of
everything, the spirit of humanitarianism works even through these
reluctant agents. For the spirit of humanitarianism is the spirit of the
age, which it is impossible for any man, born with the usual supply
of social instinct and suggestibility, completely to ignore. His reason
may tell him that his own personal advantage would be best served
if he kept the disinherited in their places. But a stronger force than
reason is for ever trying to make him act against reason. To be
utterly ruthless towards the disinherited would be profitable; but he
can never bring himself to be utterly ruthless. In spite of himself, he
feels that he ought to give them justice. And he gives it – not very
often, no doubt, and not very much at a time – but still, he gives it;
that is the queer, significant, and *modern* thing. Even in Kashmir a
tiny pinch of this humanitarian commodity – as yet, however, all but
invisible – has begun to be distributed.

Srinagar

The Mogul gardens are disappointingly inferior to any of the more
or less contemporary gardens of Italy. Shalimar and Nishat Bagh
cannot compare with the Villa d'Este at Tivoli, or the Villa Lanti,
near Viterbo. The little Chashma Shahi is architecturally the most
charming of the gardens near Srinagar. And the loveliest for trees

and waters is Atchibal, at the upper end of the valley; while far-off Verinag, where Jahangir enclosed the blue deep source of the Jhelum in an octagonal tank surrounded by arcades, has a strange and desolate beauty all its own. But in general it may be said that the design of all these Indian gardens is rigid, monotonous, and lacking entirely in the Italian grandiosity, the Italian fertility of invention. The architecture of the pleasure houses which they contain is petty and almost rustic. The decorative details, such of them, at any rate, as remain – for the ornamentation was mostly of a rather gimcrack and temporary character – are without much originality. How greatly the Mogul architects were handicapped by the profession of a religion which forbade the introduction of the human form into their decorative schemes is manifested especially in their fountains. A fountain in one of these gardens is just a nozzle sticking out of the ground, the end of a hose-pipe turned vertically upwards. Miserable object, and unworthy of the name of fountain! I shut my eyes and think of those Bolognese mermaids with their spouting breasts; those boys and tortoises at Rome, all black and shining with wetness; those naiads and river-gods and gesticulating allegories among the rainbows and the falling crystals of the Piazza Navons; those Tritons at the Villa Lanti with their prancing sea-horses – all the fantastic world of tutelary deities that stand guard over Italian springs. The Moguls were good Mohammedans and content with unadorned nozzles.

If the Kashmiri gardens are beautiful, that is the work, not so much of man as of nature. The formal beds are full of zinnias and scarlet cannas. The turf is fresh and green. The huge chenar trees go up into the pale bright sky; their white trunks shine between the leaves, which the autumn has turned to a rusty vermilion. Behind them are the steep bare hills, crested already with snow. Their colour, where the sun strikes them, is a kind of silvery-glaucous gold and, in the shadows, a deep intense indigo. Below, on the other side, stretches the Dal Lake, with the isolated fort-crowned hill of Hari-Parbat on the further shore. The sun shines out of a flawless sky, but the air is cool against the face. 'It is a nipping and an eager air'; for we are at more than five thousand feet above the sea. The Great Moguls regarded Kashmir as the earthly paradise. And a paradise to one coming fresh from the earthly hell of the Panjab in summer it must indeed have seemed. The visitor from temperate lands finds it less paradisiacal because more familiar. The lakes and mountains remind us of Switzerland and Italy, and in the level valley, with its interminable poplar avenues, its waterways, and soggy fields, we find ourselves thinking of France, of Holland even. Our ecstasies of admiration are reserved for the unfamiliar tropics.

Srinagar

In the autumn great flocks of teal and mallard come through Kashmir, on their way from the breeding-grounds to their winter home in Northern India. Some breed in the recesses of Ladakh, a few hundred miles only from the Kashmir valley; but the majority, it is said, go further afield into Central Asia, possibly even into Siberia, where so many migrants pass the brief but generous summer. In the autumn they fly southwards, over the Himalayas, into India. Some varieties of these water-fowl cross the range at the eastern end, some to the west. Thus the cotton-tail, I am assured by sportsmen, is found in Assam and Bengal, but not in the Panjab; while the mallard is seen only in the west. How these birds, which normally spend their lives in the plain, contrive to pass the Himalayas without dying of mountain-sickness or asphyxiation on the way, is something of a mystery. Most small animals, when taken up suddenly to a height of fifteen or twenty thousand feet – and many of the Himalayan passes touch these heights – simply die. The migrating duck, if it really does come down from Central Asia, must be flying at these altitudes for miles at a stretch. Physiologically, the feat seems almost as extraordinary as that of the eel, which leaves its native pond or river to breed, two or three thousand miles away, in the deep water of the ocean.

It would be interesting to know the feelings of a migrant animal, when the moment has arrived for it to perform its journey. The swallow at the end of the summer, the salmon when, having attained its maximum weight, it feels that the time has come for it to go up into the rivers, the fresh-water eel at the approach of its first and final breeding season, must feel, I imagine, much as a man might feel when suddenly converted, or who finds himself compelled by an irresistible sense of duty to perform some hazardous and disagreeable enterprise. Some power within them – an immanent god – commands them to change their comfortable way of life for a new and arduous existence. There is no disobeying the command; the god compels. If eels could formulate their theories of ethics, they would be eloquent, I am sure, about the categorical imperative and the compulsive character of the sense of duty.

Our categorical imperatives, like those of eels and swallows, are generally backed by the forces of an instinct. Our social instinct deters us from doing what we think would be condemned, and encourages us to do what we think would be commended by our equals, by our moral superiors, by our 'better selves,' by 'God.' But there are occasions, curiously enough, when the categorical imperative to do or refrain from doing seems to have no connection with a compulsive instinct. For example, a man writes two letters, addresses two envelopes, puts the letters into the envelopes, and seals them up. He is extremely careful when inserting the letters, to see that each goes into its proper envelope. Nevertheless, a few minutes later, he is seized by an irresistible desire to reopen the envelopes so as to make sure that the letter to his mistress is not in the envelope addressed to his maiden aunt, and vice versa. He knows that each letter is where it should be. But despite his conviction, despite the derisive comments of the rational part of his mind, he does reopen the envelopes. The categorical imperative is stronger than reason. It may be so strong that after five more minutes, he will open the envelopes a second time.

What gives the imperative its strength in cases such as this, I am at a loss to imagine. The August cuckoo takes wing for Africa at the command of a special migratory instinct. A desire born of his social instinct, to win the approval of his fellows, of some hypostasized 'better self' or 'personal god,' makes a man act honourably in circumstances where it would be more profitable and more convenient to act dishonourably. But when a man reopens an envelope to see if it contains the letter he *knows* it does contain, when he gets out of bed on a cold night to make sure that he has switched off the light and bolted the doors which he clearly remembers turning out and bolting ten minutes before, no primary instinct can be invoked to account for the compulsive nature of the desire to do these irrational things. In such cases the categorical imperative seems to be morally senseless and psychologically unaccountable. It is as though a god were playing practical jokes.

Srinagar

The Kashmiris are proverbial throughout India for the filthiness of their habits. Wherever a choice is offered them between cleanliness and dirt, they will infallibly choose the latter. They have a genius for filthiness. We had daily opportunities of observing the manifestations of this peculiar genius. Our compound was provided with water from the city supply. From a tap at the end of the garden we could draw the pure filtered water of the reservoir among the mountains. The water from this tap, which was left running for hours at a time, was collected in a small brick-lined tank, on which the gardener drew for the watering of his flowers. And not the gardener only. We found that our servants had an almost irresistible desire to fetch our washing and drinking water from the same source. The fresh water ran sparkling from the tap; but their instinct was to take only the standing fluid in the uncovered tank. And to what uses the tank was put! Looking out in the morning, we could see our sweeper crouching on the brink to perform his ablutions. First he washed his hands, then his feet, then his face; after that he thoroughly rinsed his mouth, gargled and spat into the tank. Then he douched his nose. And when that was finished, he scooped some water in his hands and took a drink. A yard away was the tap. He preferred the tastier water of the tank.

The astonishing thing is that epidemics are not more frequent and severe than is actually the case. That they are not is due, I suppose, to the powerful disinfectant action of the sunlight. Perhaps also an almost daily and domestic familiarity with the germs of typhoid and cholera has bred among Kashmiri phagocytes a healthy contempt for their attacks, together with increased powers of resistance.

Srinagar

The Kashmiri pandit has a more than Spanish objection to manual labour. But, unlike the hidalgo who thought himself dishonoured by the exercise of any profession save that of arms, the pandit is ambitious of wielding only the pen. He may be abjectly poor (most people are abjectly poor in Kashmir); but he will do only a pandit's work. Chauffeurs may get good wages, servants are clothed and fed; but the proud pandit had rather walk the streets begging than accept employments so derogatory to his Brahmin dignity.

There are many pandits in Kashmir. They are all educated, more or less, and all equally proud. The consequence is that, in Kashmir, you can hire a clerk for about half as much as you would have to pay your cook. And not in Kashmir only. It is the same throughout the whole of India. A circus recently visited Lahore. The management advertised for gate-keepers at fifteen rupees a month. Among the applicants, I was told, were upwards of forty graduates. Mysore, the best-governed of the Indian States, finds the same difficulty in disposing of the finished products of its higher education. After having gone to the trouble of taking their degrees, the graduates of its colleges demand, almost as a right (it is only natural), the work for which their educational attainments fit them. But the work does not exist.

That is the farcical tragedy of Indian education. The Universities produce a swarm of graduates, for whom there is nothing to do. The State can employ only a limited number of them, and, outside the government service, there is almost no opening for a man with the ordinary general education of the West. The industrial and commercial activities, to which most of our young educated men devote themselves, hardly exist in India. There is no available liquid capital to start such industries on a large scale, and the average educated Indian lacks the enterprise and energy to begin in a small way on his own. His ambition is to step into some safe clerical job with no responsibilities, and a pension at the end of it. A 'crammed' education in the humanities or in pure science hardly fits him for anything else. Unhappily, the number of safe clerkships with pensions attached is strictly limited. The Indian youth steps out of the University examination hall into a vacuum. The class of educated unemployed – the class most dangerous to an established government – steadily grows.

Srinagar

Educated Indians of the older generation have a great weakness for apophthegms, quotations, and cracker mottoes. They punctuate their conversation with an occasional 'As the Persian poet so beautifully puts it': then follows a string of incomprehensible syllables, with their appended translation, which generally embodies some such gem of human wisdon as 'Honesty is the best policy,' or 'The higher the art, the lower the morals,' or 'My uncle's house is on a hill, but I cannot eat this rotten cabbage.' Those whose education has been of a more occidental cast have *Gray's Elegy*, the works of Sir Edwin Arnold, and the more sententious parts of Shakespeare at their finger-tips. But among the younger Indians the quotation habit seems to be dying out. Their wisdom is diffuse and unquotable. Their minds are stored with the nebulous debris of newspaper articles, pamphlets, and popular science booklets, not with heroic couplets.

It is the same with us in the West. Latin tags issue from the mouths only of the aged. The days when Virgil and Horace were bandied from one side of the House of Commons to the other are past. Latin with us, like Persian among the Indians, is a deader language than it was a century, even a generation ago. Even the English classics are rarely quoted now. Young people trot out their Shakespeare less frequently than do their elders. The reason, I suppose, is this: we read so much, that we have lost the art of remembering. Indeed, most of what we read is nonsense, and not meant to be remembered. The man who remembered the social paragraphs in his morning paper would deserve to be sent to an asylum. So it comes about that we forget even that which is not worthy of oblivion. Moreover, to young people brought up in this queer provisional patchwork age of ours, and saturated with its spirit, it seems absurd to collect the rags of thought bequeathed by other and, they feel, utterly different ages. What is the use of knowing, in 1925, that 'when lovely woman stoops to folly,' the best, the only thing she can do 'is to die'? What is the good of asserting baldly that 'the quality of mercy is not strained,' that 'God's in His heaven, all's right with the world'? These poetical statements have no meaning for us. When lovely woman stoops to folly, we do not think of death; we think of suppressed complexes and birth-control and the rights of the unmarried mother. About the quality of mercy we have our own contemporary ideas; how we regard it depends on whether we are followers of Gandhi on the one hand, or of Sorel, Lenin, and Mussolini on the other. It falleth as the gentle dew from heaven; it is twice blest. No doubt. But what is this to us, who have our peculiar problems about the rights and wrongs of violence to decide in our own way? And what meaning for us have those airy assertions about God? God, we psychologists know, is a sensation in the pit of the stomach, hypostasized; God, the personal God of Browning and the modern theologian, is the gratuitous intellectual-ist interpretation of immediate psycho-physiological experiences. The experiences are indubitably true for those who feel them; but the interpretation of them in terms of Browning's personal God is illogical and unjustifiable.

No, decidedly, the cracker mottoes of the ancients are of no use to us. We need our own tags and catch-words. The preceding para-graph is full of them: complex, birth-control, violence for an idea, psychology, and the rest. Few of these words or of the ideas for which they stand have yet found their way into poetry. For example, God, the intellectually interpreted sensation in the pit of the stomach, has not yet been crystallized into couplets. His home is still the text-book, the *Hibbert Journal* article. Like most of the rest of our ideas He is unquotable. The ancients were able to build up their notions of the world at large round an elegant poetical skeleton. Less fortunate, we have only a collection of scientific, or sham-scientific, words and phrases to serve as the framework of our philosophy of life. Our minds and our conversation are consequently less elegant than those of our fathers, whose ideas had crystallized round such pleasing phrases as '*Sunt lacrimae rerum,*' 'I could not love thee, dear, so much, loved I not honour more,' and 'A sense of something far more deeply interfused.' Some day, it may be, a poet will be found to reduce our catch-words to memorable artistic form. By that time, however, they will probably be as meaninglessly out-of-date as the cracker mottoes of the classics.

Srinagar

Srinagar owns a large population of sacred cows and bulls that wander vaguely through the streets, picking up such vegetable garbage, grass, and fallen leaves as they can find. They are small beasts – the half of good-sized English cattle – and marvellously mild. Red rags mean nothing to these little bulls, they can be trusted in china shops – even in nurseries. Liberty, underfeeding, and unlimited access to the females of their species account, no doubt, for this surprising gentleness.

But, though harmless, these Hindu totems are passively a nuisance. They will not attack you as you walk or drive along the streets, but neither will they get out of your way. They stand there, meditatively ruminating, in the middle of the road, and no shouting, no ringing of bells or hooting of horns will send them away. Not until you are right on top of them will they move. The fact is, of course, that they know their own sacredness. They have learned by long experience that they can stand in the road as much as they like and that, however furiously the klaxon sounds, nothing will ever happen to them. Nothing; for Kashmir, though its inhabitants are mostly Mohammedans, is ruled by a pious Hindu dynasty. Up till a few years ago a man who killed a cow was sentenced to death. Under a milder dispensation he now gets only a matter of seven years' penal servitude. A salutary fear of cows is rooted in the breast of every Kashmiri chauffeur. And the totems know it. With a majestic impertinence they stroll along the middle of the roads. When one is a god, one does not disturb oneself for the convenience of mere man, however importunate.

To the eye of pure reason there is something singularly illogical about the way in which the Hindus shrink from killing cows or eating their flesh when dead, but have no scruples about making the life of the sacred beasts, by their ill-treatment, a hell on earth. So strict is the orthodoxy of Kashmir, that Bovril is confiscated at the frontier, and sportsmen are forbidden to shoot the wild *nilgai*, which is not bovine at all, but happens to be miscalled the 'blue cow'; the very name is sacred. And yet nothing is done to protect these god-like animals from any cruelty that does not actually result in death. They are underfed and, when used as draft animals, mercilessly overdriven. When the goad fails to make them move, their driver will seize them by the tail and, going through the motions of one who tries to start up a Ford car, violently twist. In winter, when fodder runs short, the Kashmiris pack their beasts together in a confined space until they begin to sweat, then turn them out into the snow, in the hope that they will catch pneumonia and die. To the eye of reason, I repeat it, it certainly seems strange. But then the majority of human actions are not meant to be looked at with the eye of reason.

Srinagar

It takes the Tartar traders six weeks of walking to get from Kashgar to Srinagar. They start with their yaks and ponies in the early autumn, when the passes are still free from snow and the rivers, swollen in summer by its melting, have subsided to fordableness. They walk into Kashmir, and from Kashmir into India. They spend the winter in India, sell what they have brought, and in the following spring, when the passes are once more open, go back into Turkestan with a load of Indian and European fabrics, velvet and plush and ordinary cotton, which they sell for fabulous profit in their own country.

We paid a visit to the Central Asian *sarai* at Srinagar where the Tartars halt for a rest on their way down into India. A dozen merchants with their servants were encamped there: strange Mongolian men, high-booted, trousered, jerkined in thick cloth or sheepskin. They showed us their wares: carpets, costly and cheap, from Kashgar and the other oasis cities of the Tarim basin; coarse felt mats, on which were rudely printed in red and blue the most exquisite designs; hand-woven and hand-printed cottons from Turkestan; Chinese silks, jade and crystal; furs. We bought a rug of the poorest quality, a thing of more cotton than wool, but superbly patterned in colours that were none the less beautiful for being manifestly aniline. Also a felt mat in the design of which a Greek decorative motive played a leading part. That identity of the contemporary with the ancient and classical form – was it due to the coincidence of re-invention, to a modern importation from the West? Or was it due, as I liked to think it was, to the survival, through centuries of change and tumult and in spite of invasions and slaughters, of the art which Alexander's adventurous successors, the despots of Central Asia, implanted in that once flourishing land beyond the mountains?

I do not know why it should be so; but there is something peculiarly romantic about caravans and the slow commerce of pedestrians. The spectacle of a hundred laden yaks or ponies is enough to fire the imagination; of a hundred laden trucks leaves us entirely cold. We take no interest in the merchant who sends his goods by train; but the pedestrian merchant seems to us an almost beautiful and heroic figure. And the aura of romance which surrounded the Tartars was brightened in our eyes when they showed us their medium of exchange. Diving down into the recesses of their greasy clothing, they pulled out for our inspection glittering handfuls of gold. We examined the coins. They were Russian ten-rouble pieces of before the Revolution, all bright and new. The head of the Tsar stood sharply out on them, as though they had but yesterday issued from the Imperial mint.

Taxila

The country round Taxila, that ancient city where Alexander rested and found an ally, reminded me a little of the Roman Campagna. The outworks of the Himalayas play the part of the Alban and Sabine mountains. Ranges of woodless Frascatis and desiccated Tivolis subside into a grey and rolling plain. On sudden and unexpected eminences rising out of this plain stand the Indian equivalents of Nepi and Civita Castellana. And here and there, on hill-tops, in the open ground below, lie the ruins of the various cities and temples which flourished and decayed, were born anew, only to be sacked and plundered, were re-edified, only to perish absolutely, between the year 1500 before our era and the year 500 after Christ.

First cousins, they seem – these ruins – of the tombs along the Appian Way, of Ostia and Hadrian's Villa (for ruins, whatever their date and country, have a strong family resemblance among themselves), and own brothers, I may add, to the inhabited villages near by, which differ from the ruins only in being dirtier and more dilapidated.

The best preserved remains are those of the Buddhist monastery and temple of Jaulian. The temple is a *stupa* or relic mound, and must have looked when intact, with its dome and spire of superimposed umbrellas, something like the modern Burmese pagoda – which is, of course, only a local variation of the original Indian *stupa*. To-day, nothing remains but the base of the main *stupa* with, all round it, a number of miniature *stupas* or votive shrines. The monastery adjoins the temple, and resembles almost exactly the ruins of a Christian monastery. I noticed only one point of difference: the Buddhist monks had bathrooms.

Round the base of the *stupa* and in niches in the walls of the monastic cloisters, a quantity of sculpture in stone, stucco, and clay remains intact and in position. The Greek influence is manifest, even in this work of the third century A.D. The Hellenistic leaven was active for centuries. Ages passed, and many barbarian invasions swept across the land before all traces of the Greek influence were quite eradicated and the art of Northern India became again entirely Oriental.

The quality of the work at Taxila is not particularly high. Far finer carving has been found at other sites in North-Western India. The best of it is now in the Peshawar Museum, where I was specially struck by some scenes from the life of Buddha represented in high relief on a series of small stone panels. These things have the vigour and dramatic force, with much of the beauty of composition characteristic of Italian Gothic sculpture. I remember two in particular – Buddha in the act of renouncing his family ties and

Buddha preaching from the mouth of a cave – that might have been
by Niccolo Pisano.

Between Peshawar and Lahore

At Peshawar we were seized with one of our periodical financial
panics. Money, in this country, slips rapidly between the fingers,
particularly between the fingers of the tourist. Great wads of it have
to be handed out every time one gets into the train; for fares are high
and distances enormous. No place in India seems to be less than
three hundred miles from any other place; the longer journeys have
to be measured in thousands. Financial panics are justifiable. We
decided to travel second-class as far as Lahore.

For the first hour or so we were alone in our compartment. We
congratulated ourselves on having secured all the comfort and
privacy of first-class travelling at exactly half the price. In future, we
decided, we would always travel second. But nature abhors a
vacuum, and our compartment was evidently the object of her
special abhorrence. When the train stopped at Campbellpur, we
were invaded. In the twinkling of an eye our luxurious emptiness
was filled to overflowing with luggage and humanity. And what
queer specimens of humanity! The leader of the party which now
entered the compartment was a middle-aged man wearing a yellow
robe and, on his head, a kind of quilted bonnet with hanging ear-
flaps. He was profusely garlanded with yellow chrysanthemums,
and had been followed on to the platform by a large crowd of
flower-bearing admirers and devotees. Our ignorance of the language did not permit us to discover who this exalted person might
be. But he was evidently some kind of high priest, some Hindu pope
of considerable holiness, to judge by the respect which was paid him
by his numerous retinue and his admirers. His passage along the
line must have been well advertised; for at every station our
compartment was invaded by a swarm of devotees who came to kiss
the great man's feet and to crave a blessing, which in most cases he
seemed too lazy to give. Even the guards and ticket-collectors and
stationmasters came in to pay their respects. The enthusiasm of one

ticket-collector was so great that he travelled about thirty miles in our already packed compartment, simply in order to be near the holy man. He, meanwhile, passed the time by counting his money, which was contained in a large brass-bound box, by loudly eating and, later, dozing. Even at the stations he did not take the trouble to rouse himself, but reclined with closed eyes along his seat, and passively permitted the faithful to kiss his feet. When one is as holy as he evidently was, it is unnecessary to keep up appearances, behave decently, or do anything for one's followers. Office and hereditary honour claim the respect of a believing people quite as much as personal merit.

Judging by appearances, which are often deceptive, I should say that this particular holy man had no personal merit, but a very great office. His face, which had the elements of a fine and powerful face, seemed to have disintegrated and run to fat under the influence of a hoggish self-indulgence. To look at, he was certainly one of the most repulsive human specimens I have ever seen. But of course he may in reality have been a saint and an ascetic, a preacher and a practiser of the moral doctrines formulated in the *Gita*, or even one of those pure-souled Oriental mystics who, we are told, are to leaven the materialism of our Western civilization. He may have been, but I doubt it. All that we could be certain of was that he looked unpleasant, and was undoubtedly dirty; also that he and his admirers exhaled the sour stink of garments long unwashed.

Tolstoy objected to too much cleanliness on the ground that to be too clean is a badge of class. It is only the rich who can afford the time and money to wash their bodies and shift their linen frequently. The labourer who sweats for his living, and whose house contains no bathroom, whose wardrobes no superfluous shirts, must stink. It is inevitable, and it is also right and proper, that he should. Work is prayer. Work is also stink. Therefore stink is prayer. So, more or less, argues Tolstoy, who goes on to condemn the rich for not stinking, and for bringing up their children to have a prejudice against all stinks however natural and even creditable. The non-stinker's prejudice against stink is largely a class prejudice, and therefore to be condemned.

Tolstoy is quite right, of course. We, who were brought up on open windows, clean shirts, hot baths, and sanitary plumbing, find it hard to tolerate twice-breathed air and all the odours which crowded humanity naturally exhales. Our physical education has been such that the majority of our fellow-beings, particularly those less fortunately circumstanced than ourselves, seem to us slightly or even extremely disgusting. A man may have strong humanitarian and democratic principles; but if he happens to have been brought up as a bath-taking, shirt-changing lover of fresh air, he will have to overcome certain physical repugnances before he can bring himself to put those principles into practice to the extent, at any rate, of associating freely with men and women whose habits are different from his own. It is a deplorable fact; but there it is. Tolstoy's remedy is that we should all stink together. Other reformers desire to make it economically possible for every man to have as many hot baths and to change his shirt as often as do the privileged non-stinkers at the present day. Personally, I prefer the second alternative.

Meanwhile, the crowd in our compartment increased. The day, as it advanced, grew hotter. And suddenly the holy man woke up and began to hoick and spit all over the compartment. By the time we reached Rawal Pindi we had decided that the twenty-two rupees we should economize by remaining seven hours longer among our second-class brothers were not enough. We had our luggage transferred into a first-class carriage and paid the difference. The only other occupant of the compartment was an English official of the Kashmir State, bound for his winter headquarters at Jammu. He was a dim little man; but at any rate his linen was clean, and he was not in the least holy. Nobody came in to kiss his feet.

For the rest of the journey I ruminated my anti-clericalism. Indian friends have assured me that the power of the priests is less than it was, and goes on rapidly waning. I hope they are right and that the process may be further accelerated. And not in India alone. There is still, for my taste, too much kissing of amethyst rings as well as of slippered feet. There are still too many black coats in the West, too many orange ones in the East. *Écrasez l'infâme.* My travelling companion had made me, for the moment, a thorough-going Voltairian.

It is a simple creed, Voltairianism. In its simplicity lies its

charm, lies the secret of its success – and also of its fallaciousness.
For, in our muddled human universe, nothing so simple can possibly
be true, can conceivably 'work.'

If the *infâme* were squashed, if insecticide were scattered on all the
clerical beetles, whether black or yellow, if pure rationalism became
the universal faith, all would automatically be well. So runs the
simple creed of the anti-clericals. It is too simple, and the assump-
tions on which it is based are too sweeping. For, to begin with, is the
infâme always infamous, and are the beetles invariably harmful?
Obviously not. Nor can it be said that the behaviour-value of pure
rationalism (whatever the truth-value of its underlying assump-
tions) is necessarily superior to the behaviour-value of irrational
beliefs which may be and, in general, almost certainly are untrue.
And further, the vast majority of human beings are not interested in
reason or satisfied with what it teaches. Nor is reason itself the most
satisfactory instrument for the understanding of life. Such are a few
of the complications which render so simple a formula as the anti-
clerical's inapplicable to our real and chaotic existence.

Man's progress has been contingent on his capacity to organize
societies. It is only when protected by surrounding society from
aggression, when freed by the organized labour of society from the
necessity of hunting or digging for his food, it is only, that is to say,
when society has tempered and to a great extent abolished the
struggle for personal existence, that the man of talent can exercise
his capacities to the full. And it is only by a well-organized society
that the results of his labours can be preserved for the enrichment of
succeeding generations. Any force that tends to the strengthening of
society is, therefore, of the highest biological importance. Religion is
obviously such a force. All religions have been unanimous in
encouraging within limits that have tended to grow wider and ever
wider, the social, altruistic, humanitarian proclivities of man, and in
condemning his anti-social, self-assertive tendencies. Those who like
to speak anthropomorphically would be justified in saying that
religion is a device employed by the Life Force for the promotion of
its evolutionary designs. But they would be justified in adding that
religion is also a device employed by the Devil for the dissemination
of idiocy, intolerance, and servile abjection. My fellow-passenger
from Campbellpur did something, no doubt, to encourage brotherly

love, forbearance, and mutual helpfulness among his flock. But he also did his best to deepen their congenital stupidity and prevent it from being tempered by the acquirement of correct and useful knowledge, he did his best to terrify them with imaginary fears into servility and to flatter them with groundless hopes into passive contentment with a life unworthy of human beings. What he did in the name of the evolutionary Life Force, he undid in the name of the Devil. I cherish a pious hope that he did just a trifle more than he undid, and that the Devil remained, as the result of his ministry, by ever so little the loser.

Lahore

The Lahore Museum is rich in Indo-Persian water-colours of the Mogul period. A few of them are genuinely good. But all are in the highest degree 'amusing' (and in these days, after all, it is to the amusing rather than to the good in art that we pay our tribute of admiration).

The subjects of these paintings are mostly scenes of domestic and courtly life, as it was lived in the great Imperial days. If we may judge by these representations, the distractions of the Moguls were remarkably simple, simpler even than those in vogue among the grandees of Europe at the same period. Hunting, war, and love-making, from time immemorial the sports of kings, were practised as copiously and patronized as freely by Western potentates as by their Oriental cousins. But the amusement of 'looking at the clouds' was never, so far as I am aware, a favourite pastime among the great of Europe. In India, on the contrary, it seems to have been one of the principal occupations of kings and queens. So ordinary was the pastime that the Mogul artists found it necessary to invent a special pictorial convention to represent it. These cloud-gazers, of whom quite a surprising number are portrayed in the pictures of the Lahore collection, are represented as standing or reclining on the roofs of their palaces looking up at a sky full of pitch-black vapours, against which a flight of somewhat heraldic swans stands out with a peculiar brilliance.

Innocent pleasures! The capacity to enjoy them is perhaps a sign of the superiority of Oriental civilization to our own. To Europeans, I am afraid, this 'looking at the clouds' would seem a little tedious. But then, we are barbarians and entirely ignorant of the art of living. One of the choicest inventions in the field of this epicurean art, of which we hurried Westerners know so little, is frequently represented in these pictures. It is shown in almost all the numerous love-scenes between black-bearded nawabs and fawn-eyed, trousered beauties, which form the nucleus of this delightful collection. Any fool, any savage can make love – of a kind. But it needs a *viveur* of genius to think of combining amorous dalliance – on carpets, to be added, of the most exquisite Persian design – with the leisured smoking of the silver and crystal hookah. That, surely, is true art.

Lahore

By the kindness of our hospitable friends at Lahore, we were able to hear a good deal of Indian music, both classical and popular. Indian music is innocent of any harmony more subtle than that with which the bagpipe has made us familiar – the drone on the dominant. It knows of no form more highly organized than that of the air with variations. It is played on but a few instruments (two kinds of lute and a kind of wire-stringed viola are the commonest), and these few are, alas, rapidly being ousted by a form of miniature American harmonium, pumped with one hand and played with one finger of the other. Yet, in spite of these limitations, Indian music is surprisingly rich and various. How rich and how various depends entirely upon the individual player. For in India, where music has never been committed to writing, but is an affair of tradition tempered by personal inspiration, the part of the interpreter is more important even than with us. Of European music even a bad player can give us some idea; and those who have acquired the art of reading a score can get their musical pleasure through the eye alone. Not so in India. Here the performer is all-important. He is everything; not only the interpreter, but also the repository and publisher of music – Breitkopf and Hartel as well as Paganini; not

only the guardian of ancient tradition, but also the inspired impro-
visatore. The bad performer can give you nothing of Indian music.

At Lahore, we were fortunate in hearing a most accomplished
performer on the sitar or Indian lute. He was a middle-aged man
with a walrus moustache and an explosion of most musical long
hair, in the centre of which he wore a red plush cap embroidered
with gold. He looked, I thought, like a reproduction in brown of an
old-fashioned German pianist. But how humble, in comparison with
the lordly artists of Europe, how very definitely an inferior the poor
man was! He sat on the floor awaiting our good pleasure, played
when he was told, stopped at a word in the middle of a musical
phrase, played on uncomplainingly through our conversation.
Music in India has strangely come down in the world. From being,
it is said, the accomplishment of princesses, it has come to be the
monopoly of prostitutes. Courtesans are the only professional female
musicians in India, and very many of the male professionals are only
the hereditary teachers of courtesans. Our musician had climbed a
little way above his congenital station in life; he gave lessons to
amateurs.

The sitar is a long-necked guitar, bellied with the half of a bisected
pumpkin (and having, sometimes, the second half attached like a
goitre to its neck), wire-strung, and played with a plectrum. From
this lute a skilled musician can draw an extraordinary variety of
sounds – from sharp staccato to notes long-drawn, as though
produced by a bow; from clear, full, ringing sounds to a whining
slither through fractions of a tone; from loudly martial to sweet and
tender. The melody is played only on the first string, the remaining
wires (tuned to sound the dominant, in various octaves, of the key to
whose tonic the first string is tuned) being used to produce the
accompanying drone.

Our lutanist's repertory was large, and he was prepared to play
anything we asked for. Folksongs in the pentatonic black-note scale
– first cousins, these, to what we are accustomed to regard as
characteristically Scottish airs – were followed by classical pieces, in
which the most elaborate variations were embroidered on themes
that sounded now Gregorian, now like a rambling and, to our ears,
rather tuneless Western folk-song. We heard specimens of the music
that is supposed to be played only in the morning, and specimens of

that which is intended for the night. We heard the delightful song
that is meant to be sung in cloudy weather. We heard the snake-
charmer's music, built up round a most snaky phrase of descending
semitones, and the camel-driver's song, wailing and romantic.
Generally the instrument sounded alone. But sometimes the min-
strel lifted his shaggy head and gave vent to shrill tenor notes,
neighed out from somewhere between the nose and the upper gullet.
Strange sounds, and to our ears somewhat ludicrous, particularly
when taken in conjunction with certain nods and vibrations of the
head, certain almost girlishly coquettish gestures made with a hand
that was lifted for the purpose from the sounding strings.

I was able to understand and appreciate the music tolerably well.
All of it, that is, except the music played, traditionally, when a man
gives up the world for the life of meditation. One of these renuncia-
tory pieces – a most elaborate, classical affair – was played for our
benefit. But I must confess that, listen as I might, I was unable to
hear anything particularly mournful or serious, anything specially
suggestive of self-sacrifice in the piece. To my Western ears it
sounded much more cheerful than the dance which followed it.

Emotions are everywhere the same; but the artistic expression of
them varies from age to age and from one country to another. We
are brought up to accept the conventions current in the society into
which we are born. This sort of art, we learn in childhood, is meant
to excite laughter, that to evoke our tears. Such conventions vary
with great rapidity, even in the same country. There are Elizabethan
dances that sound as melancholy to our ears as little funeral
marches. Conversely, we are made to laugh by the 'Anglo-Saxon
attitudes' of the holiest personages in the drawings and miniatures of
earlier centuries. Only with the aid of a historically trained imagination can we see or hear as our ancestors heard or saw. Remoteness in
space divides no less than remoteness in time, and to the untrained
auditor or spectator the artistic conventions of strangers are as little
comprehensible as those of his own fathers.

It is in the visual arts that the conventions for the expression of
emotions vary most widely. This is due, I suppose, to two main
causes, of a character respectively physiological and intellectual.
Form and colour have very little direct physiological effect upon the
perceiving organism. Sounds, on the other hand, act directly on the

nerves and can stimulate, exasperate, daze, bemuse, as forms and colours can never do. Certain types of rhythmical sounds produce certain almost specific effects upon the nervous system. It is obvious that in forming his conventions of expression the musician must take into account these specific physiological effects of sound. Drum-beats and loud brassy notes sounded in regular, even time are specifically exciting; it therefore follows that the convention for expressing the martial emotions can never involve slow croonings of violins in an undulating three-four time, or elaborate bird-like warblings on the flute. Thus it comes about that there is a certain family likeness common to the conventions of expression of every sytem of music – a family likeness which does not exist among the conventions of the various systems of pictorial art. But even in music the differences between the conventions of expression are very great. Music affects us physiologically through rhythm and the volume and quality of sounds. Conventions, which we have come to regard as fundamental, but which do not involve these particular factors, are found, when we compare them with the conventions of other systems, to be purely arbitrary. Thus, what we regard as the fundamental difference between major and minor keys – the minor being for us essentially melancholy – is not fundamental at all, but the result of a recent and arbitrary convention of Western musicians. Before the seventeenth century the convention did not exist even in European music, and in Oriental music it is not thought of, the most cheerful, jolly, and martial music being pitched in the minor.

So much for physiology. There are other and purely intellectual reasons why the conventions of expression should vary more widely in the different systems of visual art than they do in the systems of music. The visual arts lend themselves to story-telling and the symbolical exposition of philosophical theories and religious dogmas. Music does not. Thus, to Western eyes, the picture of a man with four arms, an elephant's head, and a lotus growing out of his navel seems grotesque. But an orthodox Hindu would see nothing comical in it. To us pictures of monsters and impossible hybrids are by convention, funny. To him they are symbolical of the highest truths.

Amritsar

The Golden Temple of the Sikhs is genuinely eighteen-carat. It is also exceedingly sacred. Holiness and costliness make up for any lack of architectural merit. For architecturally the temple is less than nothing. We went in bare-footed – the Sikhs insist on this sign of respect. Picking our way among the bird droppings and expectorated betel that strewed the causeway, we advanced gingerly towards the most golden and holiest of the shrines which stands islanded in the middle of the sacred tank. In the holy of holies three magnificent old men were chanting ecstatically to the accompaniment of a small portable harmonium, which was being played with one finger by a fourth, yet more superbly patriarchal. We listened with reverence, were offered by the verger some sugar-plums – symbolical, no doubt, of something – deposited an alms and retraced our squeamish steps along the causeway.

In the street a young beggar, half-witted, or feigning imbecility, pursued us, pitiably moaning as though he were being tortured. Bearded Akalis passed us carrying their swords. A group of male prostitutes, painted, jewelled, and dressed like women, loitered at a street corner. We turned down a narrow passage and found ourselves in the Jalianwalla Bagh, the scene of General Dyer's exploits in 1919. It is a piece of waste ground enclosed by walls and houses. The narrow passage down which we had come appeared to be the only entrance. A bad place for a crowd to be caught and fired on with machine-guns. One could kill more people here, and in a shorter time, than in most plots of ground of equal area. General Dyer proved it experimentally.

Dyer's reversion to the old-fashioned methods of Aurangzeb evoked a good deal of unfriendly comment at home. It was found shocking and un-English. At the same time, it had to be admitted that his ruthlessness had achieved what it had been intended to achieve. It put a stop to what might have turned into a revolution. The blood of the martyrs is by no means invariably the seed of the church. The victims of the Inquisition died in vain; Protestantism

disappeared from Spain as completely as the Albigensian faith from
Southern France, or as Christianity from North Africa. Persecution
can always succeed, provided that it is sufficiently violent and long-
drawn. The Romans persecuted feebly and by fits – enough to
stimulate the persecuted to fresh efforts, but not enough to destroy
them; enough to arouse sympathy for their victims, but not enough
to deter the sympathizers. That was why the blood of the early
Christian martyrs was indeed the seed of their church. If the
Romans had been as systematically ruthless as the Christians were
to show themselves in future centuries, the infant church could never
have survived. Anybody who has the power and is prepared to go on
using it indefinitely and without compunction, can force his will on
the whole world. It is obvious.

It was rarely in the past that anyone possessed of power showed
himself in the least reluctant to use it to the full. If the Romans failed
to persecute Christianity with an adequate ferocity, that was due to
their failure to realize its anti-Imperial significance, not to any
conscientious dislike to violent persecution as such. Things are
different now, at any rate in the West. Men have become reluctant
to use their power to the full, to carry authority to its logical
conclusion in brute force. Those who possessed power have volun-
tarily abstained from making full use of it, have even deprived
themselves of their power for the benefit of the powerless. Oligarchs
have granted privileges to the disinherited; industrialists have
passed laws to restrain themselves from exploiting to excess their
workmen. Instead of shooting their unwilling subjects wholesale, the
owners of colonies have dealt out constitutions. The criminal is no
longer cruelly punished, and even the domestic animal is now legally
protected from the violences of its human master.

Living as we do in the midst of this historical process, which we
vaguely call 'the humanitarian movement,' we are unable to realize
the strangeness and fundamental novelty of it. Tennyson warned us
against 'the craven fear of being great' (at other people's expense);
but the craven fear has gone on steadily growing, in spite of him.
What seems to us extraordinary to-day is not some symptom of
reluctance to use power, but its ruthless, full, and unhesitating
employment. We are amazed, not by President Wilson, but by
Mussolini; not by Chelmsford and Montagu, but by Dyer. At any

other period of the world's history than this, Dyer and Mussolini would have seemed the normal ones.

In Europe the new feelings about force and power have gradually grown up, the new policy which is the result of them has been developed by degrees. We have been brought up with them; they seem natural to us. We are too familiar with them to realize them. The anti-democratic reaction in Italy and Spain and Russia has made many of us for the first time acutely conscious of these humanitarian feelings, has rendered the nature of this democratic policy explicitly clear.

Nowhere is the contrast between old and new more striking than in India. For humanitarian feelings are not native to the Indian soil. The life of a cow, it is true, is respected, but not the life of a man. Humanitarian feelings with regard to men have been introduced artificially, from outside. And the democratic system of policy in which these feelings normally result has been grafted suddenly on another system, whose general benevolence of intention made it none the less despotic. Old and new strangely coexist, and India is ruled in accordance with two completely incompatible theories of government: that of Akbar, shall we say, and that of Woodrow Wilson. On Monday the watchword of the Executive is 'Reform and Responsible Self-Government'; like Oliver Twist, the Indians immediately ask for more; their demands become alarmingly insistent, and the Government nervously decides to be firm. On Tuesday some General Dyer rivals the exploits of the Moguls; repressive legislation is passed, the gaols are crowded. On Wednesday the Government is seized with conscientious qualms; remembering what Mr Gladstone said in 1882 and why the Great War was fought, it makes a 'generous gesture.' The response is so unenthusiastic that it becomes necessary on Thursday to suspend the Habeas Corpus Act and imprison several thousand suspects without a trial. By the end of the week, everybody, including the Government itself, is feeling rather muddled. And what about next week, and the week after that, and all the other weeks that are to follow?

Agra

I am always a little uncomfortable when I find myself unable to admire something which all the rest of the world admires – or at least is reputed to admire. Am I, or is the world the fool? Is it the world's taste that is bad, or is mine? I am reluctant to condemn myself, and almost equally reluctant to believe that I alone am right. Thus, when all men (and not the professors of English literature only, but Milton too, and Wordsworth and Keats) assure me that Spenser is a great poet, I wonder what to do. For to me Spenser seems only a virtuoso, a man with the conjuror's trick of extracting perfectly rhymed stanzas by the hundred, out of an empty mind. Perhaps I am unduly prejudiced in favour of sense; but it has always seemed to me that poets should have something to say. Spenser's is the art of saying nothing, at length, in rhyme and rumbling metre. The world admires; but I cannot. I wish I could.

Here at Agra I find myself afflicted by the same sense of discomfort. The Taj Mahal is one of the seven wonders. My guide assures me that it is 'perhaps the most beautiful building in the world.' Following its advice, we drove out to have our first look at the marvel by the light of the setting sun. Nature did its best for the Taj. The west was duly red, and orange, and yellow, and, finally, emerald green, grading into pale and flawless blue towards the zenith. Two evening stars, Venus and Mercury, pursued the sunken sun. The sacred Jumna was like a sheet of silver between its banks. Beyond it the plains stretched greyly away into the vapours of distance. The gardens were rich with turf, with cypresses, palms, and peepul trees, with long shadows and rosy lights, with the noise of grasshoppers, the calling of enormous owls, the indefatigable hammering of a coppersmith bird. Nature, I repeat, did its best. But though it adorned, it could not improve the works of man. The Taj, even at sunset, even reverberated upside down from tanks and river, even in conjunction with melancholy cypresses – the Taj was a disappointment.

My failure to appreciate the Taj is due, I think, to the fact that, while I am very fond of architecture and the decorative arts, I am very little interested in the expensive or the picturesque, as such and by themselves. Now the great qualities of the Taj are precisely those of expensiveness and picturesqueness. Milk-white amongst its dark cypresses, flawlessly mirrored, it is positively the *Toteninsel* of Arnold Boecklin come true. And its costliness is fabulous. Its marbles are carved and filigreed, are patterned with an inlay of precious stones. The smallest rose or poppy on the royal tombs is an affair of twenty or thirty cornelians, onyxes, agates, chrysolites. The New Jerusalem was not more rich in variety of precious pebbles. If the Viceroy took it into his head to build another Taj identical with the first, he would have to spend as much as a fifteenth, or even perhaps a twelfth or tenth of what he spends each year on the Indian Army. Imagination staggers . . .

This inordinate costliness is what most people seem to like about the Taj. And if they are disappointed with it (I have met several who were, and always for the same reason) it is because the building is not quite so expensive as they thought it was. Clambering among the roofs they have found evidence to show that the marble is only a veneer over cheaper masonry, not solid. It is a swindle! Meanwhile the guides and guardians are earning their money by insisting on the Taj's costliness. 'All marble,' they say, 'all precious stones.' They want you to touch as well as look, to realize the richness not with eyes alone, but intimately with the fingers. I have seen guides in Europe doing the same. Expensiveness is everywhere admired. The average tourist is moved to greater raptures by St Peter's than by his own St Paul's. The interior of the Roman basilica is all of marble. St Paul's is only Portland stone. The relative architectural merits of the two churches are not for a moment considered.

Architecturally, the worst features of the Taj are its minarets. These four thin tapering towers standing at the four corners of the platform on which the Taj is built are among the ugliest structures ever erected by human hands. True, the architect might offer a number of excuses for his minarets. He would begin by pointing out that, the dimensions of the main building and the platform being what they are, it was impossible to give the four subsidiary structures more than a certain limited mass between them, a mass small in proportion to the Taj itself. Architecturally, no doubt, it would have been best to put this definitely limited mass into four low buildings of comparatively large plan. But, unfortunately, the exigencies of religion made it necessary to put the available mass into minarets. This mass being small, it was necessary that the minarets should be very thin for their height.

These excuses, so far as they go, are perfectly valid. By the laws of religion there had to be minarets, and by the laws of proportion the minarets had to be unconscionably slender. But there was no need to make them feebly taper, there was no need to pick out the component blocks of which they are built with edgings of black, and above all there was no need to surround the shaft of the minarets with thick clumsy balconies placed, moreover, at just the wrong intervals of distance from one another and from the ground.

The Taj itself is marred by none of the faults which characterize the minarets. But its elegance is at the best of a very dry and negative kind. Its 'classicism' is the product not of intellectual restraint imposed on an exuberant fancy, but of an actual deficiency of fancy, a poverty of imagination. One is struck at once by the lack of variety in the architectural forms of which it is composed. There are, for all practical purposes, only two contrasting formal elements in the whole design – the onion dome, reproduced in two dimensions in the pointed arches of the recessed bays, and the flat wall surface with its sharply rectangular limits. When the Taj is compared with more or less contemporary European buildings in the neo-classic style of the High Renaissance and Baroque periods, this poverty in the formal elements composing it becomes very apparent. Consider, for example, St Paul's. The number of component forms in its design is very large. We have the hemispherical dome, the great colonnaded cylinder of the drum, the flat sidewalls relieved by square-faced pilasters and rounded niches; we have, at one end, the curved surfaces of the apse and, at the other, the West Front with its porch – a design of detached cylinders (the pillars), seen against a flat wall, and supporting yet another formal element, the triangular pediment. If it is argued that St Paul's is a very much larger building than the Taj, and that we should therefore expect the number of contrasting elements in its design to be greater, we may take a smaller specimen of late Renaissance architecture as our standard of comparison. I suggest Palladio's Rotonda at Vicenza, a building somewhat smaller than the Taj and, like it, of regular design and domed. Analysing the Rotonda we shall find that it consists of a far larger number of formal elements than does the Taj, and that its elegance, in consequence, is much richer, much more subtle and various than the poor, dry, negative elegance characteristic of the Indian building.

But it is not necessary to go as far as Europe to find specimens of a more varied and imaginative elegance than that of the Taj. The Hindu architects produced buildings incomparably more rich and interesting as works of art. I have not visited Southern India, where, it is said, the finest specimens of Hindu architecture are to be found. But I have seen enough of the art in Rajputana to convince me of its enormous superiority to any work of the Mohammedans. The temples at Chitor, for example, are specimens of true classicism. They are the products of a prodigious, an almost excessive, fancy, held in check and directed by the most judicious intelligence. Their elegance – and in their way they are just as elegant as the Taj – is an opulent and subtle elegance, full of unexpected felicities. The formal elements of their design are numerous and pleasingly contrasted, and the detail – mouldings and ornamental sculpture – is always, however copious, subordinated to the architectural scheme and of the highest decorative quality.

In this last respect Hindu ornament is decidedly superior to that employed by the later Moguls. The *pietra dura* work at the Taj and the Shahdara tombs at Lahore is marvellously neat in execution and of extravagant costliness. These qualities are admirable enough in their way; but they have nothing to do with the decorative value of the work considered as art. As works of art, the *pietra dura* decorations of the Taj are poor and uninteresting. Arabesques of far finer design are to be seen in the carved and painted ornamentation of Rajput palaces and temples. As for the *bas reliefs* of flowers which adorn the gateway of the Taj – these are frankly bad. The design of them vacillates uncertainly between realism and conventionalism. They are neither life-like portraits of flowers nor good pieces of free floral decoration. How any one who has ever seen a fine specimen of decorative flower-painting or flower-carving, whether Hindu or European, can possibly admire these feebly laborious reliefs passes my understanding. Indeed, it seems to me that any one who professes an ardent admiration for the Taj must look at it without having any standard of excellence in his mind – as though the thing existed uniquely, in a vacuum. But the Taj exists in a world well sprinkled with masterpieces of architecture and decoration. Compare it with these, and the Imperial Mausoleum at once takes its proper place in the hierarchy of art – well down below the best. But it is made of marble. Marble, I perceive, covers a multitude of sins.

Fatehpur Sikri

Akbar built the city as a small personal tribute to himself. The vanity of Indian potentates had a way of running to brand new cities. Witness Jai Singh's Jaipur, five miles from the existing and perfectly satisfactory town of Amber; Jodha's Jodhpur, an hour's walk from Mandor; the Udaipur of Udai Singh next door to Arh. An expensive form of royal vanity; but one for which the modern tourist should be grateful. There is nothing more picturesque than a deserted city, nothing more mournfully romantic. These deserted cities of Northern India are particularly romantic because, being relatively modern, they are all in an excellent state of preservation. For a building that is intact, but deserted, is much more romantic, more picturesquely melancholy than a deserted ruin. One expects a ruin to be deserted; nobody, it is obvious, could possibly live in Pompeii, or among the roofless remains of an English abbey. But in a building that is intact one expects to find inhabitants. When such a building is deserted, we are mournfully surprised; and the contrast between its emptiness and intactness strikes us as being strange and suggestive.

Fatehpur is less than four hundred years old, and, so far as the principal buildings are concerned, it is in a state of perfect preservation. The red sandstone which Akbar used in the building of his city is a hard, weather-resisting rock. The sculpture, the mouldings are still clean-edged and sharp. There has been no blurring of outlines, no crumbling, no leprous decay. Akbar's red city stands to-day in the condition in which he left it – and stands empty, untenanted even by the monkeys which inhabit so many of India's deserted palaces and temples.

To those whom the dry and sterile elegance of Shah Jahan's Agra has left unsatisfied, the architecture of Fatehpur Sikri will seem refreshing. For the greatest of the alien Mohammedan emperors was a patron of the indigenous Hindu art of India, and the architecture of his capital is marked by something of the genuine Hindu vigour and wealth of imagination. The *liwan* or covered portion of the mosque is particularly fine. It is divided up into three square chambers, in line and communicating; and the characteristically Hindu ceilings of these chambers are supported by a number of very tall Hindu columns. The building is superb in proportion and detail, and is certainly one of the finest pieces of interior architecture on a large scale to be seen in Upper India. And yet, such is the prestige of expensive material that poor uninteresting buildings, wholly lacking in grandeur or originality, like the Pearl Mosque at Agra, the pavilions by the lake at Ajmere, are much more widely celebrated. They are of marble; Fatehpur is only of sandstone.

It was late in the afternoon when we left the deserted city. The walls and domes glowed more rosily than ever in the light of the almost level sun. It had become a city of coral. There was a screaming in the air above us. Looking up we saw a flock of parrots flying across the pale sky. The shadow of the enormous Gate of Victory was upon them; but a moment later they emerged from it into the bright transfiguring sunlight. Over the courts of that deserted city of coral and ruddy gold a flight of emerald birds passed glittering and was gone.

Jaipur

Jaipur did not casually grow; it was made. Its streets are broad and straight, and intersect one another at right angles, like the streets of Turin or of some American city. The houses are all bright pink, and look like those charming and curiously improbable pieces of architecture in the backgrounds of Italian primitives. It is an orthodox and pious town. The pavements are thronged with ruminating bulls and Brahmins and fakirs; the shops do a thriving trade in phallic symbols, of which the manufacture, in gilt and painted marble, seems to be one of the staple industries of the place. In the streets men ride on horses, on enormous camels; or are driven in ancient victorias, in still more extraordinary four-wheelers that look like sections cut out of third-class railway coaches, or, most often, in little carts with domed canopies and (if the occupants happen to be ladies) concealing curtains, drawn by smart pairs of trotting bullocks, whose horns are painted green. Only the women of the people are visible in the streets. They move with the princely grace of those who, with pots and baskets on their heads, have passed their lives in practising the deportment of queens. Their full skirts swing as they walk, and at every step the heavy brass bangles at their feet make a loud and, oh! – for this is India – a mournfully symbolical clanking as of fetters.

Jaipur

At Jaipur we were fortunate in having an introduction to one of the great *thakurs* of the State. He was a mighty landholder, the owner of twenty villages with populations ranging from five hundred to as many thousands, a feudal lord who paid for his fief (until, a year or two ago, a somewhat simpler and more modern system of tenure was introduced) by contributing to the State army one hundred and fifty armed and mounted men. This nobleman was kind enough to place his elephant at our disposal.

It was a superb and particularly lofty specimen, with gold-mounted tusks; ate two hundredweight of food a day and must have cost at least six hundred a year to keep. An expensive pet. But for a man in the *thakur*'s position, we gathered, indispensable, a necessity. Pachyderms in Rajputana are what glass coaches were in Europe a century and a half ago – essential luxuries.

The *thakur* was a charming and cultured man, hospitably kind as only Indians can be. But at the risk of seeming ungrateful, I must confess, that, of all the animals I have ever ridden, the elephant is the most uncomfortable mount. On the level, it is true, the motion is not too bad. One seems to be riding on a small chronic earthquake; that is all. The earthquake becomes more disquieting when the beast begins to climb. But when it goes downhill, it is like the end of the world. The animal descends very slowly and with an infinite caution, planting one huge foot deliberately before the other, and giving you time between each calculated step to anticipate the next convulsive spasm of movement – a spasm that seems to loosen from its place every organ in the rider's body, that twists the spine, that wrenches all the separate muscles of the loins and thorax. The hills round Jaipur are not very high. Fortunately; for by the end of the three or four hundred feet of our climbing and descending, we had almost reached the limits of our endurance. I returned full of admiration for Hannibal. He crossed the Alps on an elephant.

We made two expeditions with the pachyderm; one – over a rocky pass entailing, there and back, two climbs and two sickening descents – to the tanks and ruined temples of Galta, and one to the deserted palaces of Amber. Emerging from the palace precincts – I record the trivial and all too homely incident, because it set me mournfully reflecting about the cosmos – our monster halted and, with its usual deliberation, relieved nature, portentously. Hardly, the operation over, had it resumed its march when an old woman who had been standing at the door of a hovel among the ruins, expectantly waiting – we had wondered for what – darted forward and fairly threw herself on the mound of steaming excrement. There was fuel here, I suppose, for a week's cooking. 'Salaam, Maharaj,' she called up to us, bestowing in her gratitude the most opulent title she could lay her tongue to. Our passage had been to her like a sudden and unexpected fall of manna. She thanked us, she blessed the great and charitable Jumbo for his Gargantuan bounty.

Our earthquake lurched on. I thought of the scores of millions of human beings to whom the passage of an unconstipated elephant seems a godsend, a stroke of enormous good luck. The thought depressed me. Why are we here, men and women, eighteen hundred millions of us, on this remarkable and perhaps unique planet? To what end? Is it to go about looking for dung – cow dung, horse dung, the enormous and princely excrement of elephants? Evidently it is – for a good many of us, at any rate. It seemed an inadequate reason, I thought, for our being here – immortal souls, first cousins of the angels, own brothers of Buddha and Mozart and Sir Isaac Newton. But a little while later I saw that I was wrong to let the consideration depress me. If it depressed me, that was only because I looked at the whole matter from the wrong end, so to speak. In painting my mental picture of the dung-searchers I had filled my foreground with the figures of Sir Isaac Newton and the rest of them. These, I perceived, should have been relegated to the remote background and the foreground should have been filled with cows and elephants. The picture so arranged, I should have been able to form a more philosophical and proportionable estimate of the dung-searchers. For I should have seen at a glance how vastly superior were their activities to those of the animal producers of dung in the foreground. The philosophical Martian would admire the dung-searchers for having discovered a use for dung; no other animal, he would point out, has had the wit to do more than manufacture it.

We are not Martians and our training makes us reluctant to think of ourselves as animals. Nobody inquires why cows and elephants inhabit the world. There is as little *reason* why we should be here, eating, drinking, sleeping, and in the intervals reading metaphysics, saying prayers, or collecting dung. We *are* here, that is all; and like other animals we do what our native capacities and our environment permit of our doing. Our achievement, when we compare it with that of cows and elephants, is remarkable. They automatically make dung; we collect it and turn it into fuel. It is not something to be depressed about; it is something to be proud of. Still, in spite of the consolations of philosophy, I remained pensive.

Jaipur

There is a mirror room in the fort at Agra; there are others in almost all the palaces of Rajputana. But the prettiest of them all are the mirror rooms in the palace of Amber. Indeed, I never remember to have seen mirrors anywhere put to better decorative use than here, in this deserted Rajput palace of the seventeenth century. There are no large sheets of glass at Amber; there is no room for large sheets. A bold and elegant design in raised plaster work covers the walls and ceiling; the mirrors are small and shaped to fit into the interstices of the plaster pattern. Like all old mirrors they are grey and rather dim. Looking into them you see 'in a glass, darkly.' They do not portray the world with that glaring realism which characterizes the reverberations of modern mirrors. But their greatest charm is that they are slightly convex, so that every piece gives back its own small particular image of the world and each, when the shutters are opened, or a candle is lit, has a glint in its grey surface like the curved high-light in an eye.

They are wonderfully rich, these mirror rooms at Amber. Their elaborateness surpasses that even of the famous mirror room at Bagheria, near Palermo. But whereas the Sicilian room is nothing more than the old-fashioned glass-and-gilding merry-go-round made stationary, the Indian rooms are a marvel of cool and elegant refinement. True, this form of decoration does not lend itself to the adornment of large areas of wall or ceiling; it is too intricate for that. But fortunately the rooms in Indian palaces are seldom large. In a country where it rains with a punctual regularity and only at one season of the year, large rooms of assembly are unnecessary. Crowds are accommodated and ceremonials of state performed more conveniently out of doors than in. The Hall of Audience in an Indian palace is a small pillared pavilion placed at one end of an open courtyard. The king sat in the pavilion, his courtiers and petitioners thronged the open space. Every room in the palace was a private room, a place of intimacy. One must not come to India expecting to find grandiose specimens of interior architecture. There are no long colonnaded vistas, no galleries receding interminably according to all the laws of perspective, no colossal staircases, no vaults so high that at night the lamplight can hardly reach them. Here in India, there are only small rooms adorned with the elaborate decoration that is meant to be looked at from close to and in detail. Such are the mirror rooms at Amber.

Bikaner

The desert of Rajputana is a kind of Sahara, but smaller and without oases. Travelling across it, one looks out over plains of brown dust. Once in every ten or twenty yards, some grey-green plant, deep-rooted, and too thorny for even camels to eat, tenaciously and with a kind of desperate vegetable ferocity struggles for life. And at longer intervals, draining the moisture of a rood of land, there rise, here and there, the little stunted trees of the desert. From close at hand the sparseness of their distantly scattered growth is manifest. But seen in depth down the long perspective of receding distance, they seem – like the in fact remotely scattered stars of the Milky Way – numerous and densely packed. Close at hand the desert is only rarely flecked by shade; but the further distances seem fledged with a dense dark growth of trees. The foreground is always desert, but on every horizon there is the semblance of shadowy forests. The train rolls on, and the forests remain for ever on the horizon; around one is always and only the desert.

Bikaner is the metropolis of this desert, a great town islanded in the sand. The streets are unpaved, but clean. The sand of which they are made desiccates and drinks up every impurity that falls upon it. And what astonishing houses flank these streets! Huge *palazzi* of red sandstone, carved and fretted from basement to attic, their blank walls – wherever a wall has been left blank – white-washed and painted with garishly ingenuous modern frescoes of horses, of battles, of trains running over bridges, of ships. These houses, the like of which we had seen in no other city, are the palaces of the Marwari merchants, the Jews of India, who go forth from their desert into the great towns, whence they return with the fruits of their business ability to their native place. Some of them are said to be fabulously wealthy, and Bikaner has, I suppose, more millionaires per thousand of population than any other town in the world.

We were shown over the country villa of one of these plutocrats, built in the desert a mile or two beyond the city wall. Costly and

unflagging labour had created and conserved in the teeth of the
sand, the scorching wind of summer and the winter frosts, a garden
of trees and lawns, of roses and English vegetables. It is the marvel
of Bikaner.

The sun was setting as we reached the bungalow. A little army of
coolies was engaged in covering the lawns with tarpaulin sheets and
fitting canvas greatcoats on all the shrubs. The night frosts are
dangerous at this season. In summer, on the other hand, it is by
day that the verdure must be jacketed. Such is horticulture in
Rajputana.

I had hoped, too optimistically, to find in the Marwari plutocrats
the modern equivalents of the Florentine merchant-princes of the
quattrocento. But this pleasing bubble of illusion burst, with an almost
audible pop, as we passed from the millionaire's garden into his
house. The principal drawing-room was furnished almost exclusively with those polychromatic *art nouveau* busts that issue from the
workshops of the tombstone manufacturers of Carrara, and with
clockwork toys. These last had all been set going, simultaneously, in
our honour. A confused ticking and clicking filled the air, and
wherever we looked our eyes were dizzied by movement. Tigers,
almost life size, nodded their heads. Pink *papier-mâché* pigs opened
and shut their mouths. Clocks in the form of fox-terriers wagged
their tails and, opening their jaws to bark, uttered a tick; in the form
of donkeys agitated their long ears sixty times a minute. And,
preciously covered by a glass dome, a porcelain doll, dressed in the
Paris fashions of 1900, jerkily applied a powder-puff to its nose, and
jerkily reached back to the powder-box – again and again. These,
evidently, are the products of our Western civilization which the
East really admires. I remembered a certain brooch which I had
seen one evening, at a dinner-party, on the *sari* of an Indian lady of
great wealth and the highest position – a brooch consisting of a disc
of blue enamel surrounded by diamonds, on the face of which two
large brilliants revolved, by clockwork, in concentric circles and
opposite directions. It was an eight-day brooch, I learned, wound
every Sunday night.

Bikaner

In the desert, five miles out of Bikaner, stands a city of tombs, the cenotaphs of the Maharajas and their royal kindred. They are to be counted by scores and hundreds – little white domes perched on pillars, or covering cells of masonry. Under each dome a little slab bears the name of the commemorated dead. In the older tombs these slabs are carved with crude reliefs, representing the prince, sometimes on horseback, sometimes sitting on his throne, accompanied by as many of his wives and concubines as burnt themselves to death on his funeral pyre. Few of these Maharajas of an earlier generation left the world without taking with them two or three unfortunate women. Some of them were accompanied to the fire by six, seven, and in one case I counted even nine victims. On the slab their images form a little frieze below the image of their lord and master – a row of small identical figures stretching across the stone. Nine luscious Hindu beauties, deep-bosomed, small-waisted, sumptuously haunched – their portraits are deliciously amusing. But looking at them, I could not help remembering the dreadful thing these little sculptures commemorated. I thought of the minutes of torment that ushered them out of life into this comical world of art which they now inhabit, under the weather-stained domes in the desert. Every here and there stands a tomb on whose central slab is carved a small conventional pair of feet. These are the feet of those royal ladies who, for one reason or another, did not commit *sati*. Each time I saw a pair of these marble feet I felt like calling for cheers.

Jodhpur

Standing on the ramparts of the Jodhpur fort – on a level with the highest wheelings of the vultures, whose nests are on the ledges of the precipices beneath the walls – one looks down on to the roofs of the city, hundreds of feet below. And every noise from the streets and houses comes floating up, diminished but incredibly definite and clear, a multitudinous chorus, in which, however, one can distinguish all the separate component sounds – crying and laughter, articulate speech, brayings and bellowings and bleatings, the creak and rumble of wheels, the hoarse hooting of a conch, the pulsing of drums. I have stood on high places above many cities, but never on one from which the separate sounds making up the great counterpoint of a city's roaring could be so clearly heard, so precisely sifted by the listening ear. From the bastions of Jodhpur fort one hears as the gods must hear from their Olympus – the gods to whom each separate word uttered in the innumerably peopled world below comes up distinct and individual to be recorded in the books of omniscience.

Jodhpur

It was late in the afternoon when we drove past the Courts of Justice. The day's business was over and the sweepers were at work, making clean for the morrow. Outside one of the doors of the building stood a row of brimming waste-paper baskets, and from these, as from mangers, two or three sacred bulls were slowly and majestically feeding. When the baskets were empty officious hands from within replenished them with a fresh supply of torn and scribbled paper. The bulls browsed on; it was a literary feast.

Watching them at their meal, I understood why it is that Indian bulls are so strangely mild. On a diet of waste-paper, it would be difficult for them to be anything but disciples of Gandhi, devotees of non-violence and *ahimsa*. I also understood why it is that Indian cows yield so little milk and, further, why the cattle of either sex are so often afflicted with hiccups. Before I came to India, I had never heard a bull hiccuping. It is a loud and terrifying sound. Hearing behind me that explosive combination of a bellow and a bark, I have often started in alarm, thinking I was on the point of being attacked. But looking round, I would find that it was only one of the mild, dyspeptic totems of the Hindus, gorged with waste-paper and painfully, uncontrollably belching as it walked.

The effects on horses of a certainly insufficient and probably also unnatural diet are different. They do not hiccup – at least I never heard them hiccuping. But as they trot the withered and emptily sagging entrails in their bellies give forth, at every step, a strange sound like the leathery creaking of organ bellows. It is a most distressing sound, but one to which all those who drive in Indian tongas must learn to accustom themselves.

Jodhpur

At the time when the question of putting an end to the East India Company's monopoly was under discussion there were several distinguished English administrators who argued that, quite apart from all considerations of commercial interests, it would be highly impolitic to open the country freely to European immigration. So far from strengthening the Company's position, they argued, the influx of Europeans would actually weaken and imperil it. For the inflowing Europeans would be commercial adventurers of no breeding or education. Now the low, when exalted by circumstances, are generally tyrannous, and the uneducated are incapable of seeing beyond the circle of their own native prejudices. In India circumstances conspire to exalt every member of the ruling race, really to some extent as well as in his own estimation. Nor is there any country in which it is more necessary to respect and make allowances for unfamiliar prejudices. Wittingly, by deliberate insult, unwittingly, by failing to allow for foreign prejudices, the low and uneducated may exasperate a subject people to whom the dominion of rulers no less foreign and in essentials no less rapacious and oppressive, but courteous and in small matters tolerant, seems comparatively unobjectionable. Open India to free European immigration and you admit into the land the potential causes of racial hatred and political unrest.

It was thus that the defenders of the Company's monopoly argued, generations ago. The case was decided against them – inevitably. It was impossible to keep India a closed country. But the supporters of lost causes are not necessarily fools. The opponents of free immigration exaggerated its dangers. But the briefest visit to India is enough to convince one that there was much truth in what they said.

At the Jodhpur dak bungalow, to which, the guest-house being full, we had been relegated, I was reminded, as I had often been reminded before, of their warnings. The reminder was more forcible than usual, since the person who reminded me was more frightfully typical of the class it was desired to exclude than any one I had hitherto met. He was ill-bred and totally uncultured; prosperous, having evidently come up in the world, and in consequence bumptious and hectoring, with all the vulgar insolence of the low man exalted and anxious to remind other people and himself of his newly acquired importance. Towards his fellow-Europeans the man's inferiority complex expressed itself in boastings; but where the Indians were concerned, it found vent, towards the poor, in bullying, towards those who looked rich enough to be able to claim the protection of the law, in insult and rudeness. Uneducated, the manifest descendant of pork butchers and publicans, he felt himself immeasurably superior to every inhabitant of the peninsula, from the Rajput prince to the pandit and the Europeanized doctor of science. He was a white man – 'one of the whitest men unhung.'

In the course of some thousands of miles of travelling in Upper India, involving many halts at station restaurants and dak bungalows, it was our misfortune to meet a good many men of this type. The Jodhpur specimen was certainly the worst, but all were bad. And all belonged to the lower orders of the unofficial, trading community.

The official class in India is composed of men of decent family, decently brought up and, as education goes, well educated. They are consequently tolerant and well behaved. For the educated man is capable of looking at things from other points of view than his own. And one who has been brought up in the ruling classes of society is generally courteous, not because he does not feel himself superior to other people, but precisely because his sense of superiority is so great that he feels that he owes it to his inferiors to be civil to them as a slight compensation for their manifest inferiority. In social intercourse it is the acts that count, not the motives behind them. The courtesy of a duke or of a royal personage charms us, and we do not reflect that it is due to a contempt for ourselves far more crushing than that which the parvenu offensively expresses for his menials and tradesmen. The blustering rudeness of the parvenu is an admission of the precariousness of his superiority. The prince is so comtemptuously certain of his, that he can afford to be civil. But civility, whatever its cause, is always civility; and rudeness angers and hurts us, even when we know it to be the expression of the sense of inferiority. The official may be courteous only because he is inwardly convinced of his enormous superiority to the Indians with whom he comes in contact; but at any rate he is courteous, and courtesy never offends. Indians may regard the official's rule as an injury to the country; but at least he refrains, generally speaking, from adding personal insult. Insult comes mainly from insignificant non-officials; it makes more enemies to English rule than official injury.

Most Englishmen who live in India will tell you that they love the Indians. For peasants, for workmen, for sepoys, for servants they feel nothing but a benevolent and fatherly affection. They greatly admire the orthodox Brahmin who thinks it wrong to cross the seas and whose learning is all mythology, Sanskrit, and a fabulous kind of history. Still greater is their admiration for the Rajput noble, that picturesque survival from the age of chivalry; he rides well, plays a good game of tennis, and is in every respect a pukka sahib – that is to say, a sportsman with good manners, a code of morals not vastly different from that current at English public schools, and no intellectual accomplishments or pretensions. The only Indians you find them objecting to as a class are those who have received a Western education. The reason is sufficiently obvious. The educated Indian is the Englishman's rival and would-be supplanter. To the slavish and illiterate masses the European is manifestly superior. Nor can the pandit, entangled in his orthodoxy and learned only in Sanskrit, the sporting nobleman, learned in nothing, ever challenge a supremacy which he owes to his Western training. All these he can afford to love, protectively. But no man loves another who threatens to deprive him of his privileges and powers. The educated Indian is not popular with the Europeans. It is only to be expected.

This dislike of the educated Indian is frequently expressed by the low European in terms of gross or covert insult. No man likes to be insulted, even by those whom he despises. Philosophers will wince at the sarcasms of passing street boys, and the unfavourable comments of critics, infinitely their inferiors, have wounded to the quick the greatest artists. It is not to be wondered at if men, who are neither sages nor geniuses and who, moreover, have been brought up in the humiliating position of members of a subject race, should be quick to resent insults. The hatred of the educated middle-class – in India, at the present time, largely unemployed and consequently embittered – is a menace to any government. In the creation of this hatred the worst bred and least educated of the Europeans have done more than their fair share.

Ajmere

The little grandson of the Indian house into which a letter of introduction had admitted us, was a child of about eight or nine, beautiful with that pure, grave, sensitive beauty which belongs only to children. In one of his books, I forget which, Benjamin Kidd has made some very judicious reflections on the beauty of children. The beauty of children, he points out, is almost a superhuman beauty. We are like angels when we are children – candid, innocently passionate, disinterestedly intelligent. The angelic qualities of our minds express themselves in our faces. In youth and earliest maturity we are human; the angel dies and we are men. Greek art, it is significant, is preoccupied almost exclusively with youth. As middle-age advances, we become less and less human, increasingly simian. Some remain ape-like to the end. Some, with the fading of the body's energies and appetites, become for a second time something more than human – the Ancients of Mr Shaw's fable, personified mind.

Ajmere

To see things – really to see them – one must use the legs as well as the eyes. Even a vicarious muscular effort quickens the vision; and a country that is looked at from horseback or a carriage, is seen almost as completely and intimately as one through which the spectator has walked on his own feet.

But there is another kind of sight-seeing, admittedly less adequate than the first, but in its own peculiar way as delightful: the sight-seeing that is done in comfort and without the contraction of a muscle from a rapidly moving machine. Railways first made it possible, to a limited extent indeed and in somewhat disagreeable conditions. The automobile has placed the whole world at the mercy of the machine, and has turned high-speed sight-seeing into a new and genuine pleasure. It is a pleasure, indeed, which the severe moralist, if he analysed it, if he were to determine exactly its mind and quality, would class, I am afraid, among the vicious pleasures; a narcotic, not an energizing pleasure; a pleasure analogous to opium-smoking; that numbs the soul and lulls it into a passive idleness; a pleasure of sloth and self-indulgence. I speak as an unrepentant addict to what I must admit to be a vice. High-speed sight-seeing induces in me a state of being like that into which one slides, one deliciously melts – alas, too rarely and for all too brief a time, at a certain stage of mild tipsiness. Sitting relaxed in the machine I stare at the slowly shifting distances, the hurrying fields and trees, the wildly fugitive details of the immediate hedgerow. Plane before plane, the successive accelerations merge into a vertiginous counterpoint of movements. In a little while I am dizzied into a kind of trance. Timelessly in the passivity almost of sleep, I contemplate a spectacle that has taken on the quality, at once unreal and vivid, of a dream. At rest I have an illusion of activity. Profoundly solitary, I sit in the midst of a phantasmagoria. I have never taken the Indian hemp, but from the depths of my trance of speed I can divine sympathetically what must be the pleasures of the hashish smoker, or the eater of bhang.

Much less completely, but satisfyingly enough, the movies have power to induce in me a similar trance. Shutting my mind to the story I can concentrate on the disembodied movement of light and shadow on the screen, until something that at last resembles the delicious hypnotism of speed descends upon me and I slide into that waking sleep of the soul, from which it is such a cruel agony to be awakened once again into time and the necessity of action.

The long days of travelling through Rajputana seemed to me, as I sat entranced at the window, at once short and eternal. The journeys occupied only as much time as it took to fall into my trance, to eat lunch and relapse, to change trains and, once more settled, to relapse again. The remaining hours did not exist, and yet were longer than thousands of years. Much passed before my eyes and was seen; but I cannot pretend that I remember a great deal of what I saw. And when I do remember, it is not so much in terms of individual objects as of processes. Innumerable separate images, seen during hours of contemplation, have blended and run together in my mind, to form a single unit of memory, just as the different phases of the growth of plants or the development of caterpillars into butterflies are selected and brought together by the photographer so as to be seen as a single brief process in a five-minute cinema film. Shutting my eyes I can revisualize, for example, the progressive changes in colour, across the breadth of Rajputana, of the horns of the oxen; how they started by being painted both green, how the green gradually melted out of one and became red, how, later, they were both red, then both parti-coloured, then finally stripped like barber's poles in concentric circles of red, white, and green. More vividly still I remember a process connected with turbans, a gradual development, the individual phases of which must have been separately observed here and there through hundreds of miles of country. I remember that they started, near Jodhpur, by being small and mostly white, that they grew larger and larger and redder and redder until, at a certain point where they came to a climax, touched an apogee of grandeur, they were like enormous balloons of dark crimson muslin with a little brown face peeping almost irrelevantly out of the middle of each. After that they began to recede again from the top of their curve. In my memory I see a process of gradual waning, culminating at Ajmere in a return to the merely normal.

The train drew up in the midst of the most ordinary Indian headwear. I had seen the rise, I had been the entranced spectator of the decline and fall of the Rajput turban. And now it was time to alight. Reluctantly, with pain I woke myself, I turned on lights inside my head, I jumped into spiritual cold baths, and at length – clothed, so to speak, and in my right mind – stepped out of my warm delicious timelessness into the noise and the grey squalor of Ajmere station.

Pushkar Lake

The holiest waters in India are mantled with a green and brilliant scum. Those who would bathe must break it, as hardy swimmers, in our colder countries, break the ice, before they can reach the spiritually cleansing liquid. Coming out of the water, bathers leave behind them jagged rifts of blackness in the green; rifts that gradually close, if no more pilgrims come down to bathe, till the green skin of the lake is altogether whole again.

There were but few bathers when we were at Pushkar. The bathing ghats going down in flights of white steps to the water were almost deserted and the hundred temples all but empty. We were able to walk easily and undisturbed along the little stone embankments connecting ghat with ghat. Here and there, on the lowest steps, a half-naked man squatted, methodically wetting himself with the scummy water, a woman, always chastely dressed, methodically soaked her clothes. On days of little concourse the bathers do not venture far out into the lake. Death lurks invisible under the green scum, swims noiselessly inshore, snaps, drags down. We saw him basking on a little shrine-crowned island a hundred yards from land, monstrous and scaly, grinning even in his sleep – a crocodile. Pushkar is so holy that no life may be taken within its waters or on its banks, not even the man-eater's. A dozen pilgrims disappear each year between those enormous jaws. It is considered lucky to be eaten by a crocodile at Pushkar.

Behind the ghats rises a charming architecture of temples and priestly houses and serais for the pilgrims – all white, with little domes against the sky, and balconies flowering out of high blank walls, and windows of lattice-work, and tunnelled archways giving a glimpse, through shadow, of sunlight beyond. Nothing very old, nothing very grand; but all exceedingly pretty, with a certain look of the Italian Riviera about it. Italian, too, are the innumerable shrines – in little niches, in ornamental sentry-boxes of stucco, under domed canopies of stone-work. Looking into them, I almost expected to see a mouldering plaster Crucifixion, an Annunciation in painted terra-cotta, a blue-robed Madonna with her Child. And it came each time as something of a shock to discover among the sacred shadows of the shrine a rough-hewn cow of marble or red sandstone, kneeling reverently before a bi-sexual phallic symbol and gazing at it with an expression on its ingenuously sculptured face of rapt ecstatic adoration.

Chitor

The fort of Chitor is larger than that of Jodhpur and therefore less spectacular. The Jodhpur fort is perched on the summit of what is almost a crag. The hill on which Chitor is built is probably as high, but it seems much lower, owing to its great length; it is a ridge, not a pinnacle of rock. And the buildings, which, at Jodhpur, are crowded into a single imposing pile, are scattered at wide intervals over the space enclosed within the circuit of the walls of Chitor. Jodhpur is wildly picturesque, like something out of a Doré picture-book. Examined at close quarters, however, it is not particularly interesting. From a distance, Chitor is less imposing; but climb up to it, and you will find it full of magnificent buildings – temples among the finest in Upper India, great ruined palaces, towers fantastically carved from base to summit. None of these buildings is much more than five hundred years old; but time has dealt hardly with them. The soft stone of which they are built has crumbled away under the rain and sun and wind. The sharp edges have become blunt, the innumerable sculptures are blurred and defaced. The splendours of Hindu art are only dimly seen, as though through an intervening mist, or with myopic and unspectacled eyes.

Chitor

Decoration is costly nowadays and money scarce. Making a virtue of economic necessity, we have proclaimed the beauty of unadorned simplicity in art. In architecture, for example, we mistrust all 'fussy details,' and can admire only the fundamental solid geometry of a building. We like our furniture plain, our silver unchased, our stage scenery flat and unconventional. Our tastes will change, no doubt, when our purses grow longer. Meanwhile, simplicity is regarded as an almost necessary quality of good art.

But the facts are against us. The best art has not been always and necessarily the simplest. Profusion of decorative detail need not obscure the main lines of the composition considered as a whole. Those who require a more convincing proof of these statements than can be found at home, should come to India. They will find in the best specimens of Hindu architecture an unparalleled extravagance of decorative details, entirely subordinated to the main architectural design. It would be difficult to find on the walls of the Chitor temples a single blank square foot. But so far from distracting the attention from the architectural composition, the sculpture and the ornament serve to emphasize the characteristic forms and movements of the strange design. If the sculpture at Chitor is unsatisfactory, that is due, not to its elaborateness and profusion, but to its poor intrinsic quality. It is all fairly good, but none of it is first-rate. The innumerable carvings at Chitor are the product of a great anonymous labour. No great original artist stands out from among the craftsmen. It is all nameless, unindividual.

Chitor

A visit to India makes one realize how fortunate, so far at any rate as the arts are concerned, our Europe has been in its religions. The Olympian religion of antiquity and, except occasionally, the

Christianity which took its place, were both favourable to the production of works of art, and the art which they favoured was, on the whole, a singularly reasonable and decent kind of art. Neither paganism nor Christianity imposed restrictions on what the artist might represent; nor did either demand of him that he should try to represent the unrepresentable. The Olympian deities were men made gods; the Saviour of the Christians was God made man. An artist could work to the greater glory of Zeus or of Jesus without ever going beyond the boundaries of real and actual human life.

How different is the state of things in India. Here, one of the two predominant religions forbids absolutely the representation of the human form, and even, where Muslim orthodoxy is strict, of any living animal form whatever. It is only occasionally, and then in purely secular art and on the smallest of scales, that this religious injunction is disobeyed. Mohammedan art tends, in consequence, to be dry, empty, barren, and monotonous.

Hinduism, on the other hand, permits the representation of things human, but adds that the human is not enough. It tells the artist that it is his business to express symbolically the superhuman, the spiritual, the pure metaphysical idea. The best is always the enemy of the good, and by trying to improve on sober human reality, the Hindus have evolved a system of art full of metaphysical monsters and grotesques that are none the less extravagant for being symbolical of the highest of 'high' philosophies. (Too high, I may add parenthetically, for my taste. Philosophies, like pheasants, can be hung too long. Most of our highest systems have been pendant for at least two thousand years. I am plebeian enough to prefer my spiritual nourishment fresh. But let us return to Hindu art.)

Readers of the *Bhagavad Gita* will remember the passage in the Eleventh Discourse, where Krishna reveals himself to Arjuna in a form hitherto unbeheld by mortal eyes: –

> 'With mouths, eyes, arms, breasts multitudinous . . .
> Long-armed, with thighs and feet innumerable,
> Vast-bosomed, set with many fearful teeth . . .'

And further: 'With many divine ornaments, with many upraised divine weapons, wearing divine necklaces and vestures, anointed with divine unguents, the God all-marvellous, boundless, with face turned every way.' And so on. The catalogue of Krishna's members, features and wardrobe covers several pages of Mrs Besant's translation of the *Gita*. We recognize the necessarily inadequate embodiment of the description in innumerable Indian statues and paintings. And what is the significance of these grotesque and repulsive monsters? Krishna himself explains it. 'Here to-day,' he says to Arjuna, 'behold the whole universe, movable and immovable, standing in one in my body.' These many-limbed monsters are symbolic, then, of the cosmos. They are the One made manifest, the All in a nutshell. Hindu artists are trying to express in terms of form what can only be expressed – and not very clearly at that, for it is difficult to speak lucidly about things of which one knows nothing – in words. The Hindus are too much interested in metaphysics and ultimate Reality to make good artists. Art is not the discovery of Reality – whatever Reality may be, and no human being can possibly know. It is the organization of chaotic appearance into an orderly and human universe.

Udaipur

By some slight error in the original introduction which made us state guests in the various capitals of Rajputana, I found myself credited, during several weeks of my tour, with the title of Professor. It was in vain that I tried to disabuse Guest Officers and Secretaries of State. I was not a professor; there were others of the same name . . . And so on. My denials were put down to an excessive modesty. Professor I remained to the last. In the end I thought it best to accept the title which had been thrust upon me. My Indian hosts preferred me to be Professor; I felt that I could not disoblige them.

Among the Indians of the older generation and in the more old-fashioned parts of the country there is a great respect for learning as such. The scholar is more highly esteemed than the artist. As a professor I found I cut more ice than as a mere writer of fiction.

The position was the same in Europe three hundred years ago. To their contemporaries, Salmasius seemed a far greater man than Milton. At the time when they came into controversy Milton was a

mere minor poet, the author of a few vernacular pieces, such as
Lycidas and *Comus*, and – more important in the eyes of the
discerning seventeenth-century public – of a number of elegant
Latin verses. Salmasius, on the other hand, was the most learned
man of his age. His commentary on Orosius was a vast mountain of
mixed rubbish raked out of the recesses of innumerable libraries. He
had read ten times as many books as any other man of his age; he
was therefore ten times as great. Whether he had profited by his
reading nobody inquired. Indeed, in any age respectful of authority,
it matters not whether a man profits by his reading or remains
throughout his life a learned ass. What is important in such an age is
the learning as such. In an age of authority originality is not valued
as highly as the capacity to repeat, parrot-like, the sayings of the
illustrious dead – even of the unillustrious; the important thing is
that they should be dead.

India is a country where tradition is strong and authority, at any
rate among the men of the older generation, is still profoundly
respected. Similar causes produce similar effects, and one can find in
India to-day the kind of scholarship that flourished in Europe up to
the end of the senventeenth century, together with a complementary
scholar-respecting public opinion. I had occasion to meet several
extremely learned men, whose attitude towards the ancient Sanskrit
literature, which was the object of their studies, was the attitude of a
scholastic towards classical and mediaeval Latin. For scholars of
this type every statement made by the ancients is true and must be
accepted without criticism. Galileo's unequal weights may fall from
the Leaning Tower in equal times. Nevertheless bodies must fall
with a speed proportional to their weight, because Aristotle says so;
and Aristotle must not be criticized or called in question. That was
the attitude towards authority in seventeenth-century Europe. And
that is still the attitude in India. You still meet in India men of
culture who accept unquestioningly anything that is written in an
ancient book. Thus, in the ancient mythological poems of India
there are certain descriptions of flying boats and chariots. Similar
references to flying are to be found in almost every mythology or
body of fairy tales; but it does not occur to us to take them seriously
as accounts of actual fact. We do not claim, for example, that Icarus
anticipated Wilbur Wright. But in India, on the other hand, these

descriptions are accepted at their face value, and I have met several intelligent and cultured men (one of them was even a scholar of some eminence) who have solemnly assured me that Zeppelins were in common use among the ancient Hindus, and that the Lord Krishna was in the habit of flying by airship to America and back.

It is obvious that, in a society where such worshippers of ancient authority still exist, it is much more respectable to be a learned than an original man, a scholar than an artist. I accepted my temporary professorship, and figuratively enthroned on the Chair of some unspecified science – for fortunately I was never pressed too closely about my subject – I carried my borrowed title with dignity and even with splendour across the kingdoms of Rajputana.

Cawnpore

Personally I have little use for political speaking. If I know something about the question at issue, I find it quite unnecessary to listen to an orator who repeats in a summarized, and generally garbled, form the information I already possess; knowing what I do, I am quite capable of making up my own mind on the subject under discussion without listening to his rhetorical persuasions. If, on the other hand, I know nothing, it is not to the public speaker that I turn for the information on which to base my judgement. The acquisition of full and accurate knowledge about any given subject is a lengthy and generally boring process, entailing the reading of many books, the collating of numerous opinions. It therefore follows, inevitably, that the imparting of knowledge can never be part of a public speaker's work, for the simple reason that if his speeches are boring and lengthy – and boring and lengthy they must be, if he is to give anything like a fair and full account of the facts – nobody will listen to him. Now it happens that I have a prejudice in favour of information. I like to know what I am doing and why. Hence, when I am ignorant, I go to the library, not to the public meeting. In the library, I know, I shall be able to collect enough facts to permit me to form an opinion of my own. At the public meeting, on the other hand, the speaker will give me only a garbled selection of the available facts, and will devote the bulk of his time and energies to persuading me by means of rhetoric to adopt his opinions. Political speaking is thus of no use to me. Either I know enough about the point at issue to make the oratory of politicians entirely superfluous; or else I know so little that their oratory is apt to be misleading and dangerous. In the first case I am in a position to make up my own mind; in the second I am not, and I do not desire to have my mind made up for me.

The All-India Congress at Cawnpore lasted for three days, and in the course of those three days I listened to more political speeches than I had previously listened to in all the years of my life. Many of them were in Hindi and therefore, to me, incomprehensible. Of the speeches in English most were eloquent; but for the reasons I have set out above they were of little use to me. If the Congress was impressive – and it did impress me, profoundly – it was not by reason of the oratory of the delegates. Oratory in large quantities is always slightly ridiculous. Particularly if it is the oratory of people who are not in a position to give effect to their words. The English in India are very quick in seeing this absurdity. Possessing as they do the power to act, they have no need to talk. It is easy for them to mock the powerless and disinherited Indians for the luxuriant copiousness of their eloquence. The Indians themselves are quite aware of the absurdity of so much oratory. 'We talk too much,' an old Indian said to me. 'But at least that's doing something. In my young days we didn't even talk.' In the beginning was the word . . . Words are creative. In the long run they have a way of generating actions. But it was not, I repeat, by the oratory that I was impressed. It was by the orators and by their audience.

Imagine an enormous tent, a hundred yards or more in length by sixty in width. Looking up, you could see, through the thin brown canvas of its roof, the shadows of wind-blown flags, and from time to time the passing silhouette of a kite or slowly soaring vulture. The floor of the tent and the platform were decently covered with matting, and it was on this matting – for there were no chairs – that the delegates sat, and sat unflinchingly, I may add, from before noon till long after sunset, six hours, seven hours and, on the last day, nearly nine. Those nine foodless hours of squatting on the floor were very nearly my last. By the time they were over, I was all but dead of sheer fatigue. But the delegates seemed positively to enjoy every moment of them. Comfort and regular meals are Western habits, which few, even of the wealthy, have adopted in the East. The sudden change to discomfort and protracted starvation is very painful to Western limbs and loins, Western hams, and Western stomachs.

It was a huge crowd. There must have been seven or eight thousand delegates packed together on the floor of the tent. In the old days, I was told, it would have been a variegated crowd of many-coloured turbans and fezes, interspersed with European hats and sun helmets. But now, since the days of non-co-operation, nobody wears anything but the white cotton 'Gandhi cap.' It is an ugly headgear, like a convict's cap. The wearers of it find the similitude symbolic. All India, they say, is one great gaol; for its inhabitants the convict's is the only suitable, the only logical uniform. From our exalted seats on the platform we looked down over what seemed a great concourse of prisoners.

It was the size of the crowd that first impressed me. Mere quantity is always impressive. The human observer is small and single. Great numbers, huge dimensions overawe him into feeling yet more solitary and minute. In the world of art even ugliness and disproportion can impress us, if there be but enough of them. The buildings which flank Victoria Street in London are architecturally monstrous; but they are so high, and the monotonous stretch of them is so long, that they end by taking on a certain grandeur. The individuals composing a Derby or Cup Final crowd may be repulsive both in appearance and character; but the crowd is none the less a magnificent and impressive thing. But at Cawnpore it was not only the quantity of humanity assembled within the Congress tent that impressed; it was its quality too. Looking through the crowd one was struck by the number of fine, intelligent faces. These faces were particularly plentiful on and in the neighbourhood of the platform, where the leaders and the more important of their followers were assembled. Whenever I remarked a particularly sensitive, intelligent or powerful face, I would make inquiries regarding its owner. In almost every case I found he had spent at least six months in gaol for a political offence. After a little practice, I learned to recognize the 'criminal type' at sight.

Cawnpore

'Pusillus, persona contemptibilis, vivacis ingenii et oculum habens perspicacem gratumque, et sponte fluens ei non deerat eloquium.' Such is William of Tyre's description of Peter the Hermit. It would serve equally well as a description of Mahatma Gandhi.

The saint of popular imagination is a person of majestic carriage, with a large intellectual forehead, expressive and luminous eyes, and a good deal of waved hair, preferably of a snowy whiteness. I do not profess to be very well up in hagiology; but my impression is that the majority of the saints about whom we know any personal details have not conformed to this ideal type. They have been more like Peter the Hermit and Mahatma Gandhi.

The qualities which make a man a saint – faith, an indomitable will, a passion for self-sacrifice – are not those that extrinsicate themselves in striking bodily stigmata. Men of great intellectual capacities generally look what they are. Sometimes it happens that these persons are further possessed of saintly qualities, and then we have the picturesque saint of popular imagination. But one can be a saint without possessing those qualities of mind which mould the face of genius into such striking and unforgettable forms.

Looking through the crowd in the Congress tent the casual observer would have been struck by the appearance of Mrs Sarojini Naidu, the President of the Congress, of Pandit Motilal Nehru, the leader of the Swarajist party. These people, he would have said, are somehow intrinsically important; their faces proclaim it. It is probable that he would never even have noticed the little man in the *dhoti*, with the shawl over his naked shoulders; the emaciated little man with the shaved head, the large ears, the rather foxy features; the quiet little man, whose appearance is only remarkable when he laughs – for he laughs with the whole-hearted laughter of a child, and his smile has an unexpected and boyish charm. No, the casual observer would probably never even have noticed Mahatma Gandhi.

Cawnpore

In the West we admire a man who fasts in order to break a world's record or win a wager; we understand his motives and can sympathize with them. But the man who goes out for forty days into the wilderness (and forty days, it may be added, are nothing in comparison with modern records), the man who fasts for the good of his soul has become incomprehensible to us. We regard him with suspicion and not, as our ancestors would have done, with reverence. So far from worshipping him, we think that he ought to be put into an asylum. With us, the ascetic, the mortifier of the flesh for the sake of the 'spirit,' the self-tormentor has ceased to command respect. We still admire the saint who gives up wealth and worldly advantage for the sake of an idea. But we demand that his sacrifice shall not be too excessive, at any rate in appearance. We deplore such visible symptoms of sainthood as the hair shirt. We do not like a saint to sacrifice, along with his money and his worldly success, his clothes, his comfort, his family ties, his marriage-bed.

In India things are different. Amongst the Hindus the enthusiasm for sainthood, even in its extremest manifestations, is as strong as it was among the Christians of the first centuries. Eloquence and energy and what is called personal magnetism are enough amongst us to make a man a successful leader of the people. But to capture the imagination of the Indian masses a man must possess, besides these qualities, the characteristics of a saint. A Disraeli can captivate the hearts of the English; he could have no sort of popular success in India. In India the most influential popular leader of modern times is Gandhi, who is a saint and an ascetic, not a politician at all. Sanctity and political astuteness are rarely combined. Gandhi's saintliness gave him power over the people; but he lacked the political ability to use that power to the best advantage.

Cawnpore

Edward Lear has a rhyme about

> an old man of Thermopylae,
> Who never did anything properly.

To the Westerner all Indians seem old men of Thermopylae. In the
ordinary affairs of life I am a bit of a Thermopylean myself. But even
I am puzzled, disquieted, and rather exasperated by the Indians. To
a thoroughly neat-minded and efficient man, with a taste for tidiness
and strong views about respectability and the keeping up of appearances, Indians must be literally maddening.

It would be possible to compile a long and varied list of what I
may call Indian Thermopylisms. But I prefer to confine my
attention to the Thermopylean behaviour of Indians in a single
sphere of activity – that of ceremonial. For it is, I think, in matters of
ceremonial and the keeping up of appearances that Indians most
conspicuously fail, in our Western opinion, 'to do anything prop-
erly.' Nobody who has looked into a temple or witnessed the
ceremonies of an Indian marriage can fail to have been struck by the
extraordinary 'sloppiness' and inefficiency of the symobolical performances. The sublime is constantly alternated with the ridiculous
and trivial, and the most monstrous incongruities are freely mingled.
The old man of Thermopylae is as busy in the palace as in the
temple; and the abodes of Indian potentates are an incredible
mixture of the magnificent and the cheap, the grandiose and the
ludicrously homely. Cows bask on the front steps; the anteroom is
filthy with the droppings of pigeons; beggars doze under the gates,
or search one another's heads for lice; in one of the inner courts fifty
courtesans from the city are singing interminable songs in honour of
the birth of the Maharaja's eleventh grandchild; in the throne room,
nobody quite knows why, there stands a brass bedstead with a sham
mahogany wardrobe from the Tottenham Court Road beside it;
framed colour prints from the Christmas number of the *Graphic* of
1907 alternate along the walls with the most exquisite Rajput and

Persian miniatures; in the unswept jewel room, five million pounds' worth of precious stones lies indiscriminately heaped; the paintings are peeling off the walls of the private apartments, a leprosy has attacked the stucco, there is a hole in the carpet; the marble hall of audience is furnished with bamboo chairs, and the Rolls Royces are driven by ragged chauffeurs who blow their noses on the long and wind-blown end of their turbans. As an Englishman belonging to that impecunious but dignified section of the upper middle-class which is in the habit of putting on dress-clothes to eat – with the most studied decorum and out of porcelain and burnished silver – a dinner of dishwater and codfish, mock duck and cabbage, I was always amazed, I was pained and shocked by this failure on the part of Eastern monarchs to keep up appearances, and do what is owing to their position.

I was even more helplessly bewildered by the Thermopylean behaviour of the delegates at the Cawnpore Congress during Mr Gandhi's speech on the position of Indians in South Africa. The applause when he ascended the rostrum was loud – though rather less loud than a Western observer might have expected. Indian audiences are not much given to yelling or hand-clapping, and it is not possible, when one is sitting on the floor, to stamp one's feet. But though the noise was small, the enthusiasm was evidently very great. And yet, when the Mahatma began to speak, there was more talking and fidgeting, more general inattention than during any other speech of the day. True, it was late in the afternoon when Mr Gandhi made his speech. The delegates had spent a long and hungry day sitting on a floor that certainly grew no softer with the passage of the hours. There was every reason for their feeling the need to relax their minds and stretch their cramped legs. But however acute its weariness had become, a Western audience would surely have postponed the moment of relaxation until the great man had finished speaking. Even if it had found the speech boring, it would have felt itself bound to listen silently and with attention to a great and admired national hero. It would have considered that chattering and fidgeting were signs of disrespect. Not so, evidently, the Indian audience. To show disrespect for the Mahatma was probably the last thing in the world that the Cawnpore delegates desired. Nevertheless they talked all through the speech, they stretched their stiff legs, they called for water, they went out for little strolls in the Congress grounds and came back, noisily. Knowing how Englishmen could comport themselves during a speech by a national hero, combining in his single person the sanctity of the Archbiship of Canterbury with the popularity of the Prince of Wales, I was astonished, I was profoundly puzzled.

In an earlier entry in this diary I attributed the Thermopylism of the Indians to a certain emotional agility (shared, to some extent, by the natives of Southern Europe), to a capacity for feeling two things at once or, at least, in very rapid succession. Indians and Neapolitans, I pointed out, can reverence their gods even while spitting, jesting, and picking their noses. But this explanation does not go far enough; it requires itself to be explained. How is it that, while we are brought up to practise consistency of behaviour, the children of other races are educated so as to be emotionally agile? Why are we so carefully taught to keep up the appearances which to others seem so negligible?

Reflecting on my observations in Italy and in India, I am led to believe that these questions must be answered in one way for the Southern Europeans, in another for the Indians. The emotional agility of the Italians is due to the profound 'realism' of their outlook, coupled with their ingrained habit of judging things in terms of aesthetics. Thus, the Southern European may admire a religious service or a royal procession as works of art, while holding strong atheistical and anti-monarchical opinions; he will be able to mock and to admire simultaneously. And perhaps he is not an atheist or a republican at all. But however ardently a Christian or a monarchist, he will always find himself able to reflect – while he kneels before the elevated Host or cheers the royal barouche – that the priest and the king make a very good thing out of their business, and that they are, after all, only human, like himself – probably all too human. As for the shabbiness and absurdities of the perform-ance, he will ignore them in his appreciation of the grandiose intention, the artistic general effect. And he will regard the Norther-ner who wants the performance to be perfect in every detail as a laborious and unimaginative fool. Nor will he understand the Northerner's passion for keeping up appearances in ordinary daily life. The Southerner has a liking for display; but his display is different from ours. When we go in for keeping up appearances, we do the job, not showily, but thoroughly, and at every point. We want all the rooms in our house to look 'nice,' we want everything in it to be 'good'; we train our servants to behave as nearly as possible like automatons, and we put on special clothes to eat even the worst of dinners. The Southerner, on the other hand, concentrates his display into a single splendid flourish. He likes to get something spectacular for his money, and his aim is to achieve, not respectability, but a work of art. He gives his house a splendid façade, trusting that every lover of the grandiose will be content to contemplate the marble front, without peering too closely at the brick and rubble behind. He will furnish one drawing-room in style, for state occasions. To keep up appearances at every point – for oneself and one's servants, as well as for the outside world – seems to him a folly and a waste of spirit. Life is meant to be enjoyed, and occasional grandiosities are part of the fun. But on ordinary days of the week it is best enjoyed in shirt sleeves.

The Indian's Thermopylisms are due, it seems to me, to entirely different causes. He is careless about keeping up appearances, because appearances seem to him as nothing in comparison with 'spiritual reality.' He is slack in the performance of anything in the nature of symbolic ceremonial, because the invisible thing symbolized seems to him so much more important than the symbol. He is a Thermopylean, not through excess of 'realism' and the aesthetic sense, but through excess of 'spirituality.' Thus the Maharaja does not trouble to make his surroundings look princely, because he feels that princeliness lies within him, not without. Marriages are made in heaven; therefore it is unnecessary to take trouble about mere marriage ceremonies on earth. And if the soul of every Indian is overflowing with love and respect for Mahatma Gandhi, why should Congress delegates trouble to give that respect the merely physical form of silence and motionlessness?

Such arguments, of course, are never consciously put. But the training of Indians is such that they act as though in obedience to them. They have been taught that this present world is more or less illusory, that the aim of every man should be to break out of the cycle of recurrent birth, that the 'soul' is everything and that the highest values are purely 'spiritual.' Owing to their early inculcation, such beliefs have tended to become almost instinctive, even in the minds of those whose consciously formulated philosophy of life is of an entirely different character. It is obvious that people holding such beliefs will attach the smallest importance to the keeping up of appearances.

In these matters we Northerners behave like Behaviourists – as though the visible or audible expression of an idea were the idea itself, as though the symbol in some sort created the notion symbolized. Our religious rites, our acts of 'natural piety,' are solemnly performed, and with an almost military precision. The impressive service, we have found, actually manufactures God; the memorial ceremony creates and conserves our interest in the dead. Our royal pageantry is no less rich, no less consistently effective; for the pageant *is* the king. Our judges are wigged and magnificently robed. Absurd survival! But no; the majesty of the law consists in the wigs and the ermine. The gentry keeps up appearances to the limit of its financial means and beyond. It is a folly, protests the believer in 'spiritual' realities. On the contrary, it is profound wisdom, based on the instinctive recognition of a great historical truth. History shows us that there were rites before there were dogmas, that there were conventions of behaviour before there was morality. Dogmas, indeed, have often been the children of rites – systems of thought called into existence to explain gestures. Morality is the theory of pre-existing social habits. (In the same way some of the greatest advances in mathematics have been due to the invention of symbols, which it afterwards became necessary to explain; from the minus sign proceeded the whole theory of negative quantities.) To sceptics desirous of believing, catholic directors of conscience prescribe the outward and visible practice of religion; practice, they know, brings forth faith; the formal appearance of religion creates its 'spiritual' essence. It is the same with civilization; men who practise the conventional ritual of civilization become civilized. Appearing to be civilized, they really are so. For civilization is nothing but a series of conventions; being civilized is obeying those conventions; is keeping up the appearance of culture, prosperity, and good manners. The more widely and the more efficiently such appearances are kept up, the better the civilization. There can never be a civilization that ignores appearances and is wholly 'spiritual.' A civilization based on

Quaker principles could not come into existence; Quakerism in all its forms is the product, by reaction, of a civilization already highly developed. Before one can ignore appearances and conventions, there must be, it is obvious, conventions and appearances to ignore. The Simple Life is simple only in comparison with some existing life of complicated convention. If Quaker principles ceased to be the luxury of a refined few, and were accepted by the world at large, civilization would soon cease to exist: freed from the necessity of keeping up the appearance of being civilized, the majority of human beings would rapidly become barbarous.

Admirers of India are unanimous in praising Hindu 'spirituality.' I cannot agree with them. To my mind 'spirituality' (ultimately, I suppose, the product of the climate) is the primal curse of India and the cause of all her misfortunes. It is this preoccupation with 'spiritual' realities, different from the actual historical realities of common life, that has kept millions upon millions of men and women content, through centuries, with a lot unworthy of human beings. A little less spirituality, and the Indians would now be free – free from foreign dominion and from the tyranny of their own prejudices and traditions. There would be less dirt and more food. There would be fewer Maharajas with Rolls Royces and more schools. The women would be out of their prisons, and there would be some kind of polite and conventional social life – one of those despised appearances of civilization which are yet the very stuff and essence of civilized existence. At a safe distance and from the midst of a network of sanitary plumbing, Western observers, disgusted, not unjustifiably, with their own civilization, express their admiration for the 'spirituality' of the Indians, and for the immemorial contentment which is the fruit of it. Sometimes, such is their enthusiasm, this admiration actually survives a visit to India.

It is for its 'materialism' that our Western civilization is generally blamed. Wrongly, I think. For materialism – if materialism means a preoccupation with the actual world in which we live – is something wholly admirable. If Western civilization is unsatisfactory, that is not because we are interested in the actual world; it is because the majority of us are interested in such an absurdly small part of it. Our world is wide, incredibly varied and more fantastic than any product of the imagination. And yet the lives of the vast majority of men and women among the Western peoples are narrow, monotonous, and dull. We are not materialistic enough; that is the trouble. We do not interest ourselves in a sufficiency of this marvellous world of ours. Travel is cheap and rapid; the immense accumulations of modern knowledge lie heaped up on every side. Every man with a little leisure and enough money for railway tickets, every man, indeed, who knows how to read, has it in his power to magnify himself, to multiply the ways in which he exists, to make his life full, significant, and interesting. And yet, for some inexplicable reason, most of us prefer to spend our leisure and our surplus energies in elaborately, brainlessly, and expensively murdering time. Our lives are consequently barren and uninteresting, and we are, in general, only too acutely conscious of the fact. The remedy is more materialism and not, as false prophets from the East assert, more 'spirituality' – more interest in this world, not in the other. The Other World – the world of metaphysics and religion – can never possibly be as interesting as this world, and for an obvious reason. The Other World is an invention of the human fancy and shares the limitations of its creator. This world, on the other hand, the world of the materialists, is the fantastic and incredible invention of – well, not in any case of Mrs Annie Besant.

Cawnpore

Some of the speeches were in Hindi, some in English. When a man began in English, there would be a shout of 'Hindi! Hindi!' from the patriots of Upper India. Those, on the other hand, who began in Hindi would find themselves interrupted by protests from the Tamil-speaking delegates of the south, who called for English. Pandit Motilal Nehru, the leader of the Swaraj party, delivered his principal oration in Hindi. When it was over, an excited man jumped up and complained to the President and the Congress at large that he had spent upwards of a hundred rupees coming from somewhere beyond Madras to listen to his leader – a hundred rupees, and the leader had spoken in Hindi; he had not understood a single word. Later in the day, one of his compatriots mounted the rostrum and retaliated on the north by making a very long and totally incomprehensible speech in Tamil. The north was furious, naturally. These are some of the minor complexities of Indian politics.

Cawnpore

The capitalist, the tax-collector, and the policeman have their places in every society, whatever its form of government. Men must work for their living, must pay for being governed, and must obey the laws. To the eye of reason, the privilege of slaving for, paying taxes to, and being put into prison by people of one's own rather than by people of another race may seem unimportant and hardly worth the trouble involved in ejecting alien policemen, tax-gatherers, and employers of labour. But men do not look at things with the eye of reason, and the Indians are men.

Whether the Indians are in a position to start governing themselves at once, whether they would do the job as well as the English, or worse, or better, I am not able to say. Nor, for that matter, is any one else. We all have our different theories about the matter; but in politics, as in science, one untested theory is as good, or as bad, as another. It is only experimentally that we can discover which out of a number of alternatives is the best hypothesis. Now the bewildering charm of politics lies in the fact that you cannot experimentally test the truth of alternative theories. At any given moment, only one choice can be made. For example, there were in 1916 certain people who held that it would be a good thing to make peace at once. There were others who thought that it would not. One cannot, it is obvious, simultaneously make peace and war. Our rulers decided in favour of war. The theory of those who thought that it would be a good thing for the world to make peace in 1916 was never tested. We know by experiment that it was an extremely bad thing to go on making war to the bitter end. To have made a premature peace might have been still worse; on the other hand, it might have been better. It remains a matter of opinion. Nobody can ever know. There is no science of politics, because there is no such thing as a political laboratory where experiments can be made.

The truth of the theories about the capacity or incapacity of the Indians to govern themselves can only be tested experimentally. There are at present merely the divergent opinions of the interested parties. I happen not to be an interested party; (for I do not consider that the mere fact of being, on the one hand, an Englishman and, on the other, a liberal with prejudices in favour of freedom and self-determination, makes me directly responsible for either the integrity of the British Empire or the liberation of the Indian people); it is easy for me to suspend judgement until the production of proof. But if I were a member of the I.C.S., or if I held shares in a Calcutta jute mill (I wish I did), I should believe in all sincerity that British rule had been an unmixed blessing to India and that the Indians were quite incapable of governing themselves. And if I were an educated Indian, I should most certainly have gone to gaol for acting on my belief in the contraries of these propositions. Moreover, even if, as an Indian, I shared the Englishman's belief, even if it could somehow be proved that Swaraj would bring, as its immediate consequences, communal discord, religious and political wars, the oppression of the lower by the higher castes, inefficiency and corruption, in a word, general anarchy – even if this could be proved, I think I should still go on trying to obtain Swaraj. There are certain things about which it is not possible, it is not right to take the reasonable, the utilitarian view.

Cawnpore

All this political talk, all this political action even – I begin to wonder, after eight and a half hours on the floor of the Congress tent, whether it isn't entirely a waste of time. Political power is the invariable concomitant of economic power. Be rich, control your country's finance and industry, and you will find that you have political leadership thrown in as a casual perquisite.

Indian industries were deliberately discouraged by the East India Company, which found itself able to make more money by selling English manufactured goods to the Indians than by selling Indian manufactured goods to the English. When, after a considerable lapse of time, modern industrialism began to be introduced into India, it was introduced under foreign auspices, and it is still, along with the Indian banking system, mainly foreign-owned. The foreigners rule; it is inevitable. But the All-India Congress goes on talking and acting in terms of politics. One might as well try to cure headaches by applying corn plasters to the toes.

Cawnpore

My prejudices happen to be in favour of democracy, self-determination, and all the rest of it. But political convictions are generally the fruit of chance rather than of deliberate choice. If I had been brought up a little differently, I might, I suppose, have been a Fascist and an apostle of the most full-blooded imperialism. But when I am honest with myself, I have to admit that I don't care two pins about political principles. Provided that it guaranteed my safety and left me in peace to do my work, I should live just as happily under an alien despotism as under the British constitution. If, in the past, men have fought for democracy and made revolutions for the attainment of self-government, it has generally been because they hoped that these things would lead to better administration than could be had under despotism and foreign dominion. Once better government has been obtained, democracy and self-determination – as such and in themselves – cease to interest those who, a short time before, had passionately fought for them.

Cawnpore

Serfs, burghers, nobles – we read about them in our history books; but we find it difficult to realize what mediaeval society was really like. To understand our European Middle Ages, one should go to India. Hereditary aristocracies will exist in the West – exist, but *pour rire*; they are scarcely more than a joke. It is in India that one learns what it meant, six hundred years ago, to be a villein, a merchant, a lord. Aristocracy, there, exists in fact, as well as in name. Birth counts. You come into the world predestined to superiority or abjection; it is a kind of social Calvinism. Some are born with Grace; they are Brahmins or Kshatriyas. The rest are damned from the beginning. Outcasts, peasants, money-lenders, merchants – the Indian hell has lower and higher circles; but even the upper circles are only the attics of the social abyss.

Almost without exception Indian politicians profess democratic principles. They envisage a popularly governed British dominion, ultimately a republic. Government by the people, for the people, and so on. But the majority of the influential ones are members of the highest castes, hereditary wise men and warriors. Their principles may be democratic, but their instincts remain profoundly aristocratic. Transplant a few mediaeval cardinals and dukes across the centuries into modern Europe; you might convince them that democracy was a good thing, but you could hardly expect them to forget from one day to the next their prejudices about villeins and burgesses, their conviction of their own inherent nobility. I have seen high-caste educated Indians treating their inferiors in a way which to a bourgeois like myself, born in even so moderately democratic a society as that of England, seemed unthinkably high-handed. I envied them the sense of assured and inalienable superiority which enabled them so naturally to play the part of the mediaeval noble.

That the lower-caste masses would suffer, at the beginning, in any case, from a return to Indian autonomy seems almost indubitable. Where the superiority of the upper classes to the lower is a matter of religious dogma, you can hardly expect the governing few to be particularly careful about the rights of the many. It is even something of a heresy to suppose that they have rights. Any indigenous government under Swaraj would necessarily be in the nature of a despotic oligarchy – that is, until education has spread so widely that another and more democratic form of government becomes practicable. One can only hope, piously, that the despotism will be paternal and that the education will spread quickly.

Cawnpore

From its advertisements much may be learned of a nation's character and habits of thought. The following brief anthology of Indian
advertisements is compiled from newspapers, magazines, medical
catalogues, and the like. Several of the most characteristic specimens
are taken from the *Cawnpore Congress Guide*, an official publication
intended for the use of delegates and interested visitors. It is with
one of these appeals to India's most enlightened public that I make a
beginning.

Beget a son and Be Happy by using the 'SON BIRTH PILLS,' my
special secret Hindu Shastrick preparation, according to directions. Ladies
who have given birth to daughters only WILL SURELY HAVE SONS NEXT, and
those who have sons MUST HAVE MALE ISSUES ONCE AGAIN by the Grace of
God. Fortunate persons desirous of begetting sons are bringing this
marvellous Something into use for brightening their dark homes and
making their lives worth their living. It is very efficacious and knows no
failure. Self praise is no recommendation. Try and be convinced. But if you
apply, mentioning this publication, with full history of your case, along with
a consultation fee of Rupees Ten (Foreign one guinea) only giving your
'Word of Honour' to give me a SUITABLE REWARD (naming the amount)
according to your means and position in life, just on the accomplishment
of your desire in due course of time, you can have the same Free,
ABSOLUTELY FREE. Act immediately, for this FREE OFFER may not remain
open indefinitely.

Here are some pleasing Hair-oil advertisements from various
sources: –

Dr ——'s Scented Almond Oil. Best preparation to be used as hair-oil for
men who do mental work. The effects of almond oil on brain are known to
everybody.
Jabukusum is a pure vegetable oil, to which medicinal ingredients and the
perfume have been added to prevent all affectations (*sic*) of the hair and the
brain.

There are several panaceas on the Indian market. There is, for
example, Sidda Kalpa Makaradhwaja which 'is a sure and infallible

specific for all Diseases, and it never fails to effect a satisfactory cure in the patient, be his ailment whatever it may. Among the various diseases amenable to its administration, to state a few, are the following:- Debility, general or nervous, including Nervous Prostration, due to whatever cause, Loss of Memory, Giddiness and Insanity . . . Asthma and Consumption, all stomach troubles . . . Cholera . . . all Kidney and Bladder Troubles . . . all Acute and Chronic Venereal Diseases . . . Leprosy of all kinds, White, Black, Red, etc. . . . Rheumatism, Paralysis, Epilepsy . . . Hysteria, Sterility . . . and all Fevers, including Malaria, Pneumonia, Influenza, and such other poisonous ones.'

Not a bad medicine, but I prefer the 'Infallible Cure for Incurable Diseases, Habits, and Defects' advertised in the *Cawnpore Guide*. The announcement runs as follows: –

I have discovered the natural system of cure for all diseases, habits, defects, failings, etc., without the use of deleterious and pernicious drugs or medicines. Being Scientific, it is absolutely safe, simple, painless, pleasant, rapid, and infallible. Diseases like hysteria, epilepsy, rheumatism, loss of memory, paralysis, insanity and mania; addiction to smoking, opium, drink, etc.; impotence, sterility, adultery, and the like can be radically cured duly by My System. Come to me after every one else has failed to do you good. I guarantee a cure in every case undertaken. Every case needs to be treated on its special merits, and so applicants should furnish me with the complete history of the health of the patient and general occupation from birth, height, measurement over chest or bust, waist and hips, and a photograph with as little dress on as possible, along with a consultation fee of Rupees Five, without which no replies can be sent.

If the buying of a postal order were not so insuperable a nuisance, I should send five rupees to get the details of the adultery cure. So much cheaper than divorce.

The following are characteristic of a large class of Indian advertisements: –

WONDERFUL WORK !!!
Works wonders in the earthly pleasure.
MARAD MITRA LAPE
Will make you a man in one day.
MARAD MITRA YAKUTI

Renews all your lost vigour and enables you to enjoy the pleasure with increased delights. Try once. 1 Bottle Rs. 10. ½ Bottle Rs 5.
FREE! FREE!!
Do you want 'Secret of Happiness from Conjugal Encounter' and 'Good Luck'? If so, apply for the illustrated literature to ——.

The enormous number of such advertisements testifies to the disastrous effect on Indian manhood of the system of child marriages. The effects, as Gandhi has pointed out in his autobiography, would probably be still worse, if it were not for the fact the Hindu girl wives generally spend at least half the year with their own parents, away from their schoolboy husbands.

The testimonials of Indian sufferers relieved by patent medicines are generally of a most lyrical character, and the oddity of the English in which they are written gives them an added charm. Here is one from an Indian Christian: –

I can say really the medicine —— is sent by Lord Jesus Christ to the sinful world to save the poor victims from their dreadful diseases. In my 8 years' experience in medical line I have come across many preparations of medicine, but I have not seen such a wonderful medicine as ——. Please send 10 phials more.

Another pious gentleman writes: –

I am living to see that I am what I am by the wonderful cure these pills wrought in me by the Grace of God, who I think has put the wisdom of preparing such pills into the head of our Venerable Pundit ——.

Another has 'no hesitation in recommending it to the suffering humanity.'
Yet another writes as follows: –

Several of my friends and myself have been using your —— for over four months for Influenza, Lumbago, Dyspepsia, Syphilis, Rheumatism and Nervous Debility with complete success. There has not been a case in which it failed. I will call it an Ambrosia.

The classical allusion is elegant and apt. One is not surprised to find that the author of the testimonial is a Bachelor of Arts.

Cawnpore

One of the evil results of the political subjection of one people by another is that it tends to make the subject nation unnecessarily and excessively conscious of its past. Its achievements in the old great days of freedom are remembered, counted over and exaggerated by a generation of slaves, anxious to convince the world and themselves that they are as good as their masters. Slaves cannot talk of their present greatness, because it does not exist; and prophetic visions of the future are necessarily vague and unsatisfying. There remains the past. Out of the scattered and isolated facts of history it is possible to build up Utopias and Cloud Cuckoo Lands as variously fantastic as the New Jerusalems of prophecy. It is to the past – the gorgeous imaginary past of those whose present is inglorious, sordid, and humiliating – it is to the delightful founded-on-fact romances of history that subject peoples invariably turn. Thus, the savage and hairy chieftains of Ireland became in due course 'the Great Kings of Leinster,' 'the mighty Emperors of Meath.' Through centuries of slavery the Serbs remembered and idealized the heroes of Kossovo. And for the oppressed Poles, the mediaeval Polish empire was much more powerful, splendid, and polite than the Roman. The English have never been an oppressed nationality; they are in consequence most healthily unaware of their history. They live wholly in the much more interesting worlds of the present – in the worlds of politics and science, of business and industry. So fully, indeed, do they live in the present, that they have compelled the Indians, like the Irish at the other end of the world, to turn to the past. In the course of the last thirty or forty years a huge pseudo-historical literature has sprung up in India, the melancholy product of a subject people's inferiority complex. Industrious and intelligent men have wasted their time and their abilities in trying to prove that the ancient Hindus were superior to every other people in every activity of life. Thus, each time the West has announced a new scientific discovery, misguided scholars have ransacked Sanskrit literature to find a phrase that might be interpreted as a Hindu anticipation of it.

A sentence of a dozen words, obscure even to the most accomplished Sanskrit scholars, is triumphantly quoted to prove that the ancient Hindus were familiar with the chemical constitution of water. Another, no less brief, is held up as the proof that they anticipated Pasteur in the discovery of the microbic origin of disease. A passage from the mythological poem of the Mahabharata proves that they had invented the Zeppelin. Remarkable people, these old Hindus. They knew everything that we know or, indeed, are likely to discover, at any rate until India is a free country; but they were unfortunately too modest to state the fact baldly and in so many words. A little more clarity on their part, a little less reticence, and India would now be centuries ahead of her Western rivals. But they preferred to be oracular and telegraphically brief. It is only after the upstart West has repeated their discoveries that the modern Indian commentator upon their works can interpret their dark sayings as anticipations. On contemporary Indian scholars the pastime of discovering and creating these anticipations never seems to pall. Such are the melancholy and futile occupations of intelligent men who have the misfortune to belong to a subject race. Free men would never dream of wasting their time and wit upon such vanities. From those who have not shall be taken away even that which they have.

Benares

A noble banyan tree stands by the side of the Jaunpur road, where it leaves the Civil Lines. Under the dense foliage lingers a kind of ecclesiastical darkness, and the rooted and already massive offshoots from the parent branches are the cathedral pillars. But the shoots which have not yet reached the ground, but hang in the dim air like the ends of aimlessly trailing cables, have an aspect strangely sinister and unholy. They hang there, motionless; and the cathedral of the banyan grove is transformed into a Piranesian prison.

The banyan is like the Hindu family. Its scions remain, even in maturity, attached to the parent tree. The national tree of England is the Oak, and English families – once, no doubt, as banyan-like as the Indian – are coming to resemble handfuls of scattered acorns that grow up at a distance from their tree of origin. Those who have had, in India or on the continent of Europe, any experience of the really united banyan family, can only feel thankful at the turn our social botany is taking.

Benares

January 14, 1926

It was said that the eclipse of the sun would be visible from Benares. But it needed more than smoked glass to see it; the eye of faith was also indispensable. That, alas, we did not possess. Partial to the point of being non-existent, the eclipse remained, for us at least, unseen. Not that we minded. For it was not to look at the moon's silhouette that we had rowed out that morning on the Ganges; it was to look at the Hindus looking at it. The spectacle was vastly more extraordinary.

There were, at the lowest estimate, a million of them on the bathing ghats that morning. A million. All the previous night and day they had been streaming into the town. We had met them on every road, trudging with bare feet through the dust, an endless and silent procession. In bundles balanced on their heads they carried provisions and cooking utensils and dried dung for fuel, with the new clothes which it is incumbent on pious Hindus to put on after their bath in honour of the eclipsed sun. Many had come far. The old men leaned wearily on their bamboo staves. Their children astride of their hips, the burdens on their heads automatically balanced, the women walked in a trance of fatigue. Here and there we would see a little troop that had sat down to rest – casually, as is the way of Indians, in the dust of the road and almost under the wheels of the passing vehicles.

And now the day and the hour had come. The serpent was about to swallow the sun. (It was about to swallow him in Sumatra, at any rate. At Benares it would do no more than nibble imperceptibly at the edge of his disk. The serpent, should one say, was going to try to swallow the sun.) A million of men and women had come together at Benares to assist the Light of Heaven against his enemy.

The ghats go down in furlong-wide flights of steps to the river, which lies like a long arena at the foot of enormous tiers of seats. The tiers were thronged to-day. Floating on the Ganges, we looked up at acres upon sloping acres of humanity.

On the smaller and comparatively unsacred ghats the crowd was a little less densely packed than on the holiest steps. It was at one of these less crowded ghats that we witnessed the embarkation on the sacred river of a princess. Canopied and curtained with glittering cloth of gold, a palanquin came staggering down through the crowd on the shoulders of six red-liveried attendants. A great barge, like a Noah's ark, its windows hung with scarlet curtains, floated at the water's edge. The major-domo shouted and shoved and hit out with his rod of office; a way was somehow cleared. Slowly and with frightful lurchings, the palanquin descended. It was set down, and in the twinkling of an eye a little passage-way of canvas had been erected between the litter and the door of the barge. There was a heaving of the cloth of gold, a flapping of the canvas; the lady – the ladies, for there were several of them in the litter – had entered the barge unobserved of any vulgar eye. Which did not prevent them, a few minutes later when the barge had been pushed out into mid-stream, from lifting the scarlet curtains and peering out with naked faces and unabashed curiosity at the passing boats and our inquisitive camera. Poor princesses! They could not bathe with their plebeian and unimprisoned sisters in the open Ganges. Their dip was to be in the barge's bilge-water. The sacred stream is filthy enough under the sky. What must it be like after stagnating in darkness at the bottom of an ancient barge?

We rowed on towards the burning ghats. Stretched out on their neat little oblong pyres, two or three corpses were slowly smoulder-ing. They lay on burning faggots, they were covered by them. Gruesomely and grotesquely, their bare feet projected, like the feet of those who sleep uneasily on a bed too short and under exiguous blankets.

A little further on we saw a row of holy men, sitting like cormorants on a narrow ledge of masonry just above the water. Cross-legged, their hands dropped limply, palm upwards, on the ground beside them, they contemplated the brown and sweating tips of their noses. It was the Lord Krishna himself who, in the *Bhagavad*

Gita, prescribed that mystic squint. Lord Krishna, it is evident, knew all that there is to be known about the art of self-hypnotism. His simple method has never been improved on; it puts the mystical ecstasy *à la portée de tous*. The noise of an assembled million filled the air; but no sound could break the meditative sleep of the nose-gazers.

At a given moment the eye of faith must have observed the nibblings of the demoniacal serpent. For suddenly and simultaneously all those on the lowest steps of the ghats threw themselves into the water and began to wash and gargle, to say their prayers and blow their noses, to spit and drink. A numerous band of police abbreviated their devotions and their bath in the interest of the crowds behind. The front of the waiting queue was a thousand yards wide; but a million people were waiting. The bathing must have gone on uninterruptedly the whole day.

Time passed. The serpent went on nibbling imperceptibly at the sun. The Hindus counted their beads and prayed, made ritual gestures, ducked under the sacred slime, drank, and were moved on by the police to make room for another instalment of the patient million. We rowed up and down, taking snapshots. West is West.

In spite of the serpent, the sun was uncommonly hot on our backs. After a couple of hours on the river, we decided that we had had enough, and landed. The narrow lanes that lead from the ghats to the open streets in the centre of the town were lined with beggars, more or less holy. They sat on the ground with their begging bowls before them; the charitable, as they passed, would throw a few grains of rice into each of the bowls. By the end of the day the beggars might, with luck, have accumulated a square meal. We pushed our way slowly through the thronged alleys. From an archway in front of us emerged a sacred bull. The nearest beggar was dozing at his post – those who eat little sleep much. The bull lowered its muzzle to the sleeping man's bowl, made a scouring movement with its black tongue, and a morning's charity had gone. The beggar still dozed. Thoughtfully chewing, the Hindu totem turned back the way it had come and disappeared.

Being stupid and having no imagination, animals often behave far more sensibly than men. Efficiently and by instinct they do the right, appropriate thing at the right moment – eat when they are hungry, look for water when they feel thirst, make love in the mating season, rest or play when they have leisure. Men are intelligent and imaginative; they look backwards and ahead; they invent ingenious explanation for observed phenomena; they devise elaborate and roundabout means for the achievement of remote ends. Their intelligence, which has made them the masters of the world, often causes them to act like imbeciles. No animal, for example, is clever and imaginative enough to suppose that an eclipse is the work of a serpent devouring the sun. That is the sort of explanation that could occur only to the human mind. And only a human being would dream of making ritual gestures in the hope of influencing, for his own benefit, the outside world. While the animal, obedient to its instinct, goes quietly about its business, man, being endowed with reason and imagination, wastes half his time and energy in doing things that are completely idiotic. In time, it is true, experience teaches him that magic formulas and ceremonial gestures do not give him what he wants. But until experience has taught him – and he takes a surprisingly long time to learn – man's behaviour is in many respects far sillier than that of the animal.

So I reflected, as I watched the sacred bull lick up the rice from the dozing beggar's bowl. While a million people undertake long journeys, suffer fatigue, hunger, and discomfort in order to perform, in a certain stretch of very dirty water, certain antics for the benefit of a fixed star ninety million miles away, the bull goes about looking for food and fills its belly with whatever it can find. In this case, it is obvious, the bull's brainlessness causes it to act much more rationally than its masters.

To save the sun (which might, one feels, very safely be left to look after itself) a million of Hindus will assemble on the banks of the Ganges. How many, I wonder, would assemble to save India? An immense energy which, if it could be turned into political channels, might liberate and transform the country, is wasted in the name of imbecile superstitions. Religion is a luxury which India, in its present condition, cannot possibly afford. India will never be free until the Hindus and the Moslems are as tepidly enthusiastic about their religion as we are about the Church of England. If I were an Indian millionaire, I would leave all my money for the endowment of an Atheist Mission.

Lucknow

At the end of the second day of the All-India Musical Conference, I declared a strike. Accustomed to the ordinary three-hour day of the European concert-goer, I found myself exhausted by the seven or eight hours of daily listening imposed on me by the makers of the Lucknow programme. There was one long concert every morning, another every afternoon, a third at night. It was too much. After the second day I would not go again. Still, before I struck, I had had sixteen hours of Indian music – enough, at home, to hear all the symphonies of Beethoven with a good sprinkling of characteristic specimens from Mozart and Bach thrown in. Sixteen hours of listening should be enough to give one at least the hang of an unfamiliar music.

Professional musicians, mostly attached to the courts of reigning princes, had come to Lucknow from every part of India. There were accomplished singers and celebrated players of every Indian instrument – including even the harmonium, which, to my great astonishment and greater disgust, was permitted to snore and whine in what I was assured was the very sanctuary of Indian music. I listened to all the virtuosity of India. That it touched me less than the more modest accomplishment of the old Lahore musician was due, I think, to purely physical causes. The vina and the sitar must be heard at close quarters. All the expression and feeling that a performer puts into his playing evaporates at a distance, and nothing can be heard beyond the jangle of the plucked strings. At Lahore I had been amazed by the richness and variety of the tone that came out of the old musician's sitar. At Lucknow, where the concerts were held in a large tent, I was wearied by its tinkling monotony. Space had sucked the soul out of the music; it came to me dry and dead.

Much is enthusiastically talked about the use of quarter-tones in Indian music. I listened attentively at Lucknow in the hope of hearing some new and extraordinary kind of melody based on these celebrated fractions. But I listened in vain. The scales in which

Indian music is written are of quite familiar types. The pentatonic or black-note scale, for example, seems to be a favourite; and any one learned in ancient European music would probably find no difficulty in labelling with their modal names the various melodies of India. The quarter-tone makes its appearance only in the slurred transition from one note of the fundamental scale to another. The sentimental tzigane violinist and the jazz-band player make just as free a use of quarter-tones as do the Indians, and in precisely the same way.

Lucknow

There was an All-India Art Exhibition at Lucknow as well as an All-India Musical Conference. Some of the pictures were ancient, some contemporary. The old were not conspicuously interesting specimens, the modern, I regret to say, were incredibly bad. I do not exaggerate when I say that there was no contemporary exhibitor at Lucknow who showed the smallest trace of artistic ability. I can only suppose that, for one reason or another, those Indians who have talent do not become artists. Of the men exhibiting at Lucknow, most, I noticed, were teachers in Government Art Schools, and therefore the last people in the world one would expect to be artists. The others were mostly patriotic amateurs who thought that modern India ought to have a national art of its own and had set out to create it. The intention was laudable. But in art, alas, intentions and high moral purpose count for very little. It is the talent that matters, and talent was precisely the thing that none of them possessed.

Lucknow

At the Lucknow hotel the coffee, instead of being undrinkable in the familiar Britannic way, was made of chicory. I sipped, and instantaneously all France was present to me – the whole of it at once and through twenty years of history. The Reims of last year with the

Chamonix of 1907, Grenoble before the War, Fontainebleau in 1925, Paris at every date from the opening of the Edwardian era onwards. Within its own particular Gallic sphere that drop of liquid chicory was as miraculously efficacious as the Last Trump. The dead sprang to life, were visible and spoke – in French. There was a resurrection of French landscapes and French monuments. Forgotten incidents re-enacted themselves for me, against a French background: dead pleasures and miseries, dead shames and elations experienced within the boundaries of France, shot up, like so many Jacks-in-the-box, from under suddenly lifted tombstones. I finished my breakfast in France and in the past, and walked abroad. At the end of remembered and phantasmal boulevards loomed up the relics of the Indian Mutiny and the gimcrack palaces of the Kings of Oudh. Dark-faced and turbaned, an Indian policeman walked clean through the tenuous ghosts of friends and lovers. Gradually the resurrected died again; the tombstones closed on graves that were once more tenanted. The present had conquered the past; at an impact from outside the inward world had fallen to pieces. I addressed myself to the enjoyment of immediate pleasures. But I looked forward to to-morrow's breakfast; the chicory, I felt sure, would repeat the miracle. These resuscitators of the past, these personal Last Trumps may be relied on, if they are not abused, to produce a constant and invariable effect. There is a certain tune (by Sousa, I think) which I can never hear without remembering my convalescence at school after an attack of mumps. I remember myself looking out of a window, and humming the tune, interminably, for hours, feeling as I did so profoundly, but most enjoyably, miserable – goodness knows why. And then, still more mysteriously moving, there is a certain smell, occasionally mingled with the smoke of autumn bonfires; a smell that is due to the combustion of some exotic rubbish, but rarely mingled with the ordinary muck, and whose identity I have never been able to trace; a strange, sweetish smell, like the unhealthy caricature of a scent; a smell that every time I sniff it reminds me urgently and agonizingly of something in my past life, some cardinal incident, some crisis, some turning point, which I know to be profoundly significant, but which I am chronically unable to recall. What is more irritating than to find a knot in one's handkerchief, to be reminded that the commission was desperately important, and to find oneself incapable of remembering what it was? I have a feeling that if only I could remember what that bonfire smell reminded me of, I should be perceptibly nearer to solving the problem of the universe. But my best efforts have always proved unavailing. I have a fear that I shall never remember.

Delhi

The Viceroy's speech at the opening of the Legislative Assembly was mainly official and expository. But it contained a few more moving passages of the few-well-chosen-words variety. His voice trembling – a trifle studiedly – with suppressed emotion, His Excellency professed himself 'grieved' that the Indian response to Lord Birkenhead's 'generous gesture' (I think those were the words) had been so inadequate. I have forgotten whether he actually went on to speak about England's self-appointed task of preparing India for self-government. All that I can be certain of is that the overtones of his speech were loud with the White Man's Burden.

There was a time when I should have preferred to this rather snuffling enunciation of pious hopes and high ideals a more brutally 'realistic' outburst in the manner of Mussolini. But that was long ago. I have outgrown my boyish admiration for political cynicism and am now an ardent believer in hypocrisy. The political hypocrite admits the existence of values higher than those of immediate national, party, or economic interest. Having made the admission, he cannot permit his actions to be too glaringly inconsistent with his professed principles. With him there are always 'better feelings' to be appealed to. But the realist, the political cynic, has no 'better feelings.' A Mussolinian Viceroy would simply say: 'We are here primarily for our own profit, not for that of the inhabitants of the country. We have immense force at our disposal and we propose to use it ruthlessly in order to keep what we have won. In no circumstances will we give away any of our power.' To such a man it is obviously useless to talk about democracy, self-determination, the brotherhood of man. He does not profess to feel the slightest respect for any of these ideas; why should he act as though he did? A politician who professes to believe in humanitarianism can always be reminded of his principles. He may not sincerely or thoroughly believe in them – though no man professes principles in which he has no belief whatever – but having made professions, he is afraid of acting in a manner too wildly inconsistent with them.

The more cant there is in politics, the better. Cant is nothing in itself; but attached to even the smallest quantity of sincerity, it serves, like a nought after a numeral, to multiply whatever of genuine goodwill may exist. Politicians who cant about humanitarian principles find themselves sooner or later compelled to put those principles into practice – and far more thoroughly than they had ever originally intended. Without political cant there would be no democracy. Pecksniff, however personally repulsive, is the guardian of private morality. And if it were not for the intellectual snobs who pay – in solid cash – the tribute which philistinism owes to culture, the arts would perish with their starving practitioners. Let us thank heaven for hypocrisy.

Delhi

Re-reading the preceding paragraph, I wonder why I wrote it. No cant, no democracy: therefore, let there be cant. The implication, of course, is that democracy is something excellent, an ideal to be passionately wished for. But, after all, is democracy really desirable? European nations certainly do not seem to be finding it so at the moment. And even self-determination is not so popular as it was. There are plenty of places in what was once the Austrian Empire where the years of Habsburg tyranny are remembered as a golden age, and the old bureaucracy is sincerely regretted. And what is democracy, anyhow? Can it be said that government by the people exists anywhere, except perhaps in Switzerland? Certainly, the English parliamentary system cannot be described as government by the people. It is a government of oligarchs for the people and with the people's occasional advice. Do I mean anything whatever when I say that democracy is a good thing? Am I expressing a reasoned opinion? Or do I merely repeat a meaningless formula by force of habit and because it was drummed into me at an early age? I wonder. And that I am able to wonder with such a perfect detachment is due, of course, to the fact that I was born in the upper-middle, governing class of an independent, rich, and exceedingly powerful nation. Born an Indian or brought up in the slums of London, I should hardly be able to achieve so philosophical a suspense of judgement.

Delhi

The Legislative Assembly, passes a great many resolutions. The Government acts on about one in every hundred of them. Indians are not very enthusiastic about their budding parliament. It is not, perhaps, to be wondered at. Indian politicians find it useful, I suppose, because they can talk more violently within the Chamber than without. The violent speeches are reported in the press. It is all good propaganda, no doubt. But it is nothing more. The Government members are, of course, well aware that it is nothing more. Some do not even take the trouble to conceal their knowledge, but adopt throughout the sittings of the Assembly a consistently flippant attitude of amused and secure superiority.

Delhi

The wars of Troy had their Homer. But other and more significant events, other cities vastly greater, have remained uncommemorated in the outer darkness that lies beyond the frontiers of the little luminous world of art. Men, places, and happenings do not always and necessarily get the chroniclers they deserve. Shakespeare is without his Boswell and his Holbein. The European War has not, as yet at any rate, produced its Tolstoy or its Goya. No Swift has reacted to modern America. Nor, finally, has contemporary Delhi, nor the new India of which it is the capital and epitome, evolved its Marcel Proust.

How often, while at Delhi, I thought of Proust and wished that he might have known the place and its inhabitants. For the imperial city is no less rich in social comedy than Paris; its soul is as fertile in snobberies, dissimulations, prejudices, hatreds, envies. Indeed, I should say that in certain respects the comedy of Delhi is intrinsically superior to that which Proust found in the Faubourg Saint-Germain and so minutely analysed. The finest comedy (I speak for the moment exclusively as the literary man) is the most serious, the most nearly related to tragedy. The comedy of Delhi and the new India, however exquisitely diverting, is full of tragic implications. This dispute of races, the reciprocal hatred of colours, the subjection of one people to another – these things lie behind its snobberies, conventions, and deceits, are implicit in every ludicrous antic of the comedians. Sometimes, when a thunderstorm is approaching, we may see a house, a green tree, a group of people illuminated by a beam of the doomed sun, and standing out with a kind of unearthly brightness against the black and indigo of the clouds. The decaying relics of feudalism, the Dreyfus case, the tragedies of excessive leisure – these form the stormy background to the Proustian comedy. The clouds against which imperial Delhi appears so brilliantly comical, are far more black, far more huge and menacing.

In India I was the spectator of many incidents that might have come straight out of '*A la Recherche du Temps Perdu*'; trivial incidents, but pregnant with the secret passions and emotions which Proust could always find, when they were there, beneath the most ordinary gestures, the most commonplace and innocuous words. I remember, for example, the behaviour of an Indian guest at a certain hotel, where the European manager made a habit of strolling about the dining-room during meals, superintending the service, chatting with the diners and, when they rose to leave, opening the door to let them out. The Indian, I noticed, never gave the manager a chance of opening the door for him. When he wanted to leave the dining-room, he would wait till the manager's back was turned and then fairly run to the door, turn the handle and slip through, as though the devil were after him. And indeed the devil *was* after him – the devil in the form of a painful suspicion that, if he gave the manager an opportunity of opening the door for him, the fellow might make a humiliating exception to his rule of courtesy and leave it conspicuously shut.

I remember a dinner-party at Delhi, at which the embarrassment was all on the other side. An Indian politician was the host; the guests, two other politicians, a high English official, and ourselves. It was a cheerful evening. With the roast, the Indians began talking of the time they had spent in gaol during the Non-Co-operation Movement. It had been for them a not too uncomfortable and even rather comical experience. They were men of standing; it was only natural that they should have been exceptionally well treated. 'Besides,' the eldest and most eminent of the politicians explained, parodying the words of a Great Mogul, 'rivers of champagne had flowed between me and Sir ——, who was the governor of the province.' Rivulets, one gathered, continued to flow, even in the prison. The conversation was entirely good-humoured, and was punctuated with laughter. But the English official listened with a certain embarrassment. He was, after all, a member of the executive which had had these men thrown into gaol; and the fact that they had, on the whole, enjoyed themselves in prison did not diminish his indirect responsibility for their having been sent there. Nor were the comments of the Indians on the paternal and imprisoning government any the less scathing for being uttered with a laugh of good-natured derision. I did not envy the official; his situation was dreadfully ticklish. He was a guest, to begin with; moreover, the post he had occupied since the introduction of the Montford Reforms officially imposed upon him a behaviour towards Indian politicians of more than ordinary courtesy and cordiality. He existed, officially, to make the Legislative Assembly work; he was there to lubricate the ill-designed and creaking machinery of Indian parliamentary government. It was impossible for him either in his public or his private capacity to protest against the remarks of the Indian politicians. At the same time it was no less impossible for him, as a member of the British executive, to accept or agree with them. He adopted the only possible course, which was to disassociate himself completely from the conversation, to be as though he were not. He did it, I must say, marvellously well; so well, indeed, that there was a certain moment (the Government was catching it particularly hot) when he seemed on the point of becoming invisible, of fading out altogether, like the Cheshire Cat. I admired his tact and thanked God that I was not called upon to exercise it. The lot of the modern I.C.S. official is not entirely enviable.

And then there were the Maharajas. The Chamber of Princes –
that remarkable assembly, attended every year by a steadily dimin-
ishing number of Indian rulers – was holding its sittings while we
were at Delhi. For a week Rolls Royces were far more plentiful in the
streets than Fords. The hotels pullulated with despots and their
viziers. At the Viceroy's evening parties the diamonds were so large
that they looked like stage gems; it was impossible to believe that the
pearls in the million-pound necklaces were the genuine excrement of
oysters. How hugely Proust would have enjoyed the Maharajas!
Men with a pride of birth more insensate than that of Charlus;
fabulously rich, and possessing in actual fact all the despotic power
of which the name of Guermantes is only the faint hereditary
symbol; having all the idiosyncrasies and eccentricities of Proust's
heroes and none of their fear of public opinion; excessive and
inordinate as no aristocrat in the modern West could hope to be;
carrying into Napoleonic or Neronian actuality the poor potential
velleities towards active greatness or vice that are only latent in men
who live in and not above society. He would have studied them with
a passionate interest, and more especially in their relations – their
humiliating and gravely ludicrous relations – with the English. It
would have charmed him to watch some Rajput descendant of the
Sun going out of his way to be agreeable to the official who, though
poor, insignificant, of no breeding, is in reality his master; and the
spectacle of a virtuous English matron, doing her duty by making
polite conversation to some dark and jewelled Heliogabalus, notor-
ious for the number of his concubines and catamites, would have
delighted him no less. How faithfully he would have recorded their
words, how completely and with what marvellous intuition he would
have divined the secret counterpoint of their thoughts! He would
have been deeply interested, too, in that curious unwritten law
which decrees that European women shall dance in public with no
Indian below the rank of Raja. And it would, I am sure, have
amused him to observe the extraordinary emollient effect upon even
the hardest anti-Asiatic sentiments of the possession of wealth and a
royal title. The cordiality with which people talk to the dear
Maharaja Sahib – and even, occasionally, about him – is delightful.
My own too distant and hurried glimpses of the regal comedies of
India made me desire to look more lingeringly, more closely, and

with a psychological eye acuter than that with which nature has grudgingly endowed me.

I remember so many other pregnant trifles – the pathetic gratitude of a young man in an out-of-the-way place, to whom we had been ordinarily civil, and his reluctance to eat a meal with us, for fear that he should eat it in an un-European fashion and so eternally disgrace himself in our eyes. The extraordinarily hearty, back-slapping manner of certain educated Indians who have not yet learned to take for granted their equality with the ruling Europeans and are for ever anxious loudly to assert it. The dreadfully embarrassing cringing of others. The scathing ferocity of the comments which we overheard, in the gallery of the Legislative Assembly, being made on the Indian speakers by the women-folk of certain Government members. Listening, I was reminded of the sort of things that were said by middle-class people in England about the workmen at the time of the coal strike. People whose superiority is precarious detest with passion all those who threaten it from below.

Nor must I forget – for Proust would have devoted a score of pages to it – the noble Anglo-Indian convention of dressing for dinner. From the Viceroy to the young clerk, who, at home, consumes high tea at sunset, every Englishman in India solemnly 'dresses.' It is as though the integrity of the British Empire depended in some directly magical way upon the donning of black jackets and hard-boiled shirts. Solitary men in dak bungalows, on coasting steamers, in little shanties among the tiger-infested woods, obey the mystical imperative and every evening put on the funereal uniform of English prestige. Women, robed in the latest French creations from Stratford-atte-Bowe, toy with the tinned fish, while the mosquitoes dine off their bare arms and necks. It is magnificent.

Almost more amazing is that other great convention for the keeping up of European prestige – the convention of eating too much. Five meals a day – two breakfasts, luncheon, afternoon tea, and dinner – are standard throughout India. A sixth is often added in the big towns where there are theatres and dances to justify late supper. The Indian who eats at the most two meals a day, sometimes only one – too often none – is compelled to acknowledge his inferiority. In his autobiography Gandhi records his youthful lapses – after what frightful wrestlings with his conscience! – into meat eating. A fellow-schoolboy led him into the sin. Meat, the tempter speciously argued, was the secret of English supremacy. The English were strong because they ate so much. If Indians would stuff themselves as imperially, they would be able to turn the English out of India. Gandhi was struck; he listened, he allowed himself to be convinced. He ate – three or four times, at least. Perhaps that is why he came as near as he did to turning the English out of India. In any case, the story proves how deeply the Indians are impressed by our gastronomic prowess. Our prestige is bound up with overeating. For the sake of the Empire the truly patriotic tourist will sacrifice his liver and his colon, will pave the way for future apoplexies and cancers of the intestine. I did my best while I was in India. But at the risk of undermining our prestige, of bringing down the whole imperial fabric in ruins about my ears, I used from time to time unobtrusively to skip a course. The spirit is willing, but the flesh, alas, is weak.

Calcutta

Indian industrial workers are recruited from the villages. Tradition is strong in the villages, and the rules of conduct are religiously and therefore ruthlessly enforced. When the pressure from outside is relaxed and they find themselves enjoying an unfamiliar freedom in the slums of the great cities, these industrialized countrymen tend to go, morally, to pieces.

Contact with strangers who play the game of life according to unfamiliar rules tends to weaken the compulsive force of commandments which, in the village, are unquestioningly obeyed. For moralities, however excellent and efficient each may be when alone, are mutually destructive. They are like spiders – cannibals of their own kind. Brought into contact in the mind of a simple man, they will devour one another and leave him without any morality at all. And while it weakens the countryman's powers of resisting criminal temptations, city life at the same time multiplies the opportunities of profitable crime. In the village, where the actions of each individual are known to all the others, honesty, chastity, and temperance are the best policy. In the slums of a huge city, where every man is, so to speak, anonymous and solitary in the crowd, they may easily cease to be profitable. The honest, domestic, and temperate countryman is too often transformed by contact with the town into a thievish and fornicating drunkard.

The disturbing effects of a sudden change of environment on even the tolerably well-educated are always and everywhere apparent. On their first arrival in Paris young English and American men will behave as they would never dream of behaving at home. Young women, too, one is forced to add. It was ever so. St Boniface writing to the then Archbishop of Canterbury complained that: 'perpaucae sunt civitates in Longobardia vel in Francia aut in Gallia, in qua non sit adultera vel meretrix generis Anglorum, quod scandalum est et turpitudo totius ecclesiae vostrae.' That was in A.D. 745; but the Saint might have been prophetically describing the state of things in 1926. The modern Italians tell an anecdote about a foreigner who asked a Florentine acquaintance why there were so few light and complaisant ladies to be found in his otherwise admirable city. The Florentine shrugged his shoulders. 'Abbiamo le Americane,' he explained. The story is doubtless untrue; but it is significant that it should ever have been invented.

In India the importance to the individual of his community with its traditional religion, its traditional code of rules, is vastly greater than it is in the West. Deprived of these supports, the Indian finds it hard to stand. On him, therefore, the effect of a change of environment from the village to the distant city is generally much more serious than it would be to a Westerner.

The growth of industrialism in India has been accompanied by a corresponding break-up of rural community life. Up to the present, however, industrialism has made but small progress in India, and village life as a whole is almost intact. But a beginning has been made, and we may divine from Calcutta, Bombay, and Cawnpore what a largely industrialized India might become. The prophetic vision is not particularly inspiring. But material conditions may be improved, and I like to think that the emancipation of a section of the population from the bonds of community life may prove in the end to be spiritually healthful. Up till now, as any one who knows the slums of Indian industrial towns will tell you, emancipation has only been harmful. But in time, perhaps, the urbanized peasant will learn to accommodate himself to liberty. Freed from communal restraints, he may learn to develop his own personal resources in a manner hitherto unknown in rural India, where the human unit has always been the community, not the individual man or woman.

It is a pleasing hope and one which, as a lover of freedom and of change, a hater of fixity and ready-made commandments, a believer in individuals, and an infidel wherever groups, communities and crowds are concerned, I cherish with a peculiar fondness. Hinduism and the Indian village system have been praised on the score that they have preserved the Indian people and the Indian character, have kept them unaltered and the same through centuries of physical assault and spiritual battery. To me the achievement seems more worthy of blame than of praise. Fixity is appalling. It is better, it seems to me, to be destroyed, to become something unrecognizably different, than to remain for ever intact and the same, in spite of altering circumstance.

But these, no doubt, are jejune and romantic prejudices, born of false notions regarding the end and aim of human existence – of what is perhaps the first and fundamental false notion that human existence has any aim or end whatever, beyond its own prolongation and reproduction. To one who believes that man is here on earth to adventure, to know, to try all things, to advance (if only for the fun of advancing, of not standing still) towards some quite unattainable goal of perfection, the Indian scheme of existence will seem unsatisfactory in the extreme. But if man (which may in reality be the case) is born only that he may live for a little, beget offspring, and die to make room for those he has begotten, then the Indian village community will seem the almost perfect form of social organization. In an Indian village men can scratch up a living, breed, and die, without wasting a particle of their energy on vain experiments, on the pursuit of ideal will-o'-the-wisps, on the making of progress foredoomed by nature and man's own destructiveness to lead nowhere. The only real flaw that I can discover in Indian village life is that it is profoundly boring. Change, incessant experiment, the hunt for knowledge are interesting. That is the best, perhaps the only, justification for these things.

That human beings will ever be able to dispense altogether with the Indian village or its equivalent seems doubtful. Man needs something outside himself to hang on to – a stable society, a system of conventions, a house, a piece of land, possessions, a family. Already in the most completely urbanized and industrialized parts of our world we can find migrant populations of men and women, who live in no place long enough to become attached to it or influenced by its spirit, who own no land, nor any tangible possessions – only the convenient symbol of money – who have few or no children, who believe in no organized religion. These people are being compelled, by their mode of life, to impose an enormous strain on their own resources of mind and will, on personal relationships with their fellows – on love, marriage, friendship, family ties. They have nothing solid, outside themselves, on which they can lean. The strain they impose on them is often more than their spiritual resources and their personal relationships will bear. Hence a dissatisfaction, a shallowness of life, a profound uncertainty of purpose.

I have always felt a passion for personal freedom. It is a passion which the profession of writing has enabled me to gratify. A writer is his own master, works when and where he will, and is paid by a quite impersonal entity, the public, with whom it is unnecessary for him to have any direct dealings whatever.

Professionally free, I have taken care not to encumber myself with the shackles that tie a man down to one particular plot of ground; I own nothing, nothing beyond a few books and the motor-car which enables me to move from one encampment to another.

It is pleasant to be free, when one has enough to do and think about to prevent one's ever being bored, when one's work is agreeable and seems (pleasing illusion!) worth while, when one has a clear conception of what one desires to achieve and enough strength of mind to keep one, more or less undeviatingly, on the path that leads to this goal. It is pleasant to be free. But occasionally, I must confess, I regret the chains with which I have not loaded myself. In these moods I desire a house full of stuff, a plot of land with things growing on it; I feel that I should like to know one small place and its people intimately, that I should like to have known them for years, all my life. But one cannot be two compatible things at the same time. If one desires freedom, one must sacrifice the advantages of being bound. It is, alas, only too obvious.

Calcutta

Any given note of a melody is in itself perfectly meaningless. A melody is an organism in time, and the whole, or at least a considerable proportion of the whole, must be heard, through an appropriate duration, before the nature of the tune can be discovered. It is, perhaps, the same with life. At any given moment life is completely senseless. But viewed over a long period, it seems to reveal itself as an organism existing in time, having a purpose, tending in a certain direction. That life is meaningless may be a lie so far as the whole of life is concerned. But it is the truth at any given instant. The note, A natural, is in itself insignificant. But the note A natural, when combined in a certain way with a certain number of other notes, becomes an essential part of the 'Hymn to Joy' in Beethoven's *Choral Symphony*. It is conceivable that the moment of world existence, of which we are each aware during a human lifetime, may be an essential part in a musical whole that is yet to be unfolded. And do the notes which we have already deciphered in the records of history and geology justify us in supposing that we are living a melody – a melody almost infinitely prolonged? It is a matter of opinion.

Calcutta

The experimenter's is a curious and special talent. Armed with a tea canister and some wire, with silk, a little sealing-wax, and two or three jam-pots, Faraday marched forth against the mysterious powers of electricity. He returned in triumph with their captured secrets. It was just a question of suitably juxtaposing the wax, the glass jars, the wires. The mysterious powers couldn't help surrendering. So simple – if you happened to be Faraday.

And if you happened to be Sir J. C. Bose, it would be so simple, with a little clockwork, some needles and filaments, to devise machines that would make visible the growth of plants, the pulse of their vegetable 'hearts,' the twitching of their nerves, the processes of their digestion. It would be so simple – though it cost even Bose long years of labour to perfect his instruments.

At the Bose Institute in Calcutta, the great experimenter himself was our guide. Through all an afternoon we followed him from marvel to marvel. Ardently and with an enthusiasm, with a copiousness of ideas that were almost too much for his powers of expression and left him impatiently stammering with the effort to elucidate methods, appraise results, unfold implications, he expounded them one by one. We watched the growth of a plant being traced out automatically by a needle on a sheet of smoked glass; we saw its sudden, shuddering reaction to an electric shock. We watched a plant feeding; in the process it was exhaling minute quantities of oxygen. Each time the accumulation of exhaled oxygen reached a certain amount, a little bell, like the bell that warns you when you are nearly at the end of your line of typewriting, automatically rang. When the sun shone on the plant, the bell rang often and regularly. Shaded, the plant stopped feeding; the bell rang only at long intervals, or not at all. A drop of stimulant added to the water in which the plant was standing set the bell wildly tinkling, as though some record-breaking typist were at the machine. Near it – for the plant was feeding out of doors – stood a large tree. Sir J. C. Bose told us that it had been brought to the garden from a distance. Transplanting is generally fatal to a full-grown tree; it dies of shock. So would most men if their arms and legs were amputated without an anaesthetic. Bose administered chloroform. The operation was completely successful. Waking, the anaesthetized tree immediately took root in its new place and flourished.

But an overdose of chloroform is as fatal to a plant as to a man. In one of the laboratories we were shown the instrument which records the beating of a plant's 'heart.' By a system of levers, similar in principle to that with which the self-recording barometer has made us familiar, but enormously more delicate and sensitive, the minute pulsations which occur in the layer of tissue immediately beneath the outer rind of the stem, are magnified – literally millions of times – and recorded automatically in a dotted graph on a moving sheet of smoked glass. Bose's instruments have made visible things that it has been hitherto impossible to see, even with the aid of the most powerful microscope. The normal vegetable 'heart beat,' as we saw it recording itself point by point on the moving plate, is very slow. It must take the best part of a minute for the pulsating tissue to pass from maximum contraction to maximum expansion. But a grain of caffeine or of camphor affects the plant's 'heart' in exactly the same way as it affects the heart of an animal. The stimulant was added to the plant's water, and almost immediately the undulations of the graph lengthened out under our eyes and, at the same time, came closer together: the pulse of the plant's 'heart' had become more violent and more rapid. After the pick-me-up we administered poison. A mortal dose of chloroform was dropped into the water. The graph became the record of a death agony. As the poison paralysed the 'heart,' the ups and downs of the graph flattened out into a horizontal line half-way between the extremes of undulation. But so long as any life remained in the plant, this medial line did not run level, but was jagged with sharp irregular ups and downs that represented in a visible symbol the spasms of a murdered creature desperately struggling for life. After a little while, there were no more ups and downs. The line of dots was quite straight. The plant was dead.

The spectacle of a dying animal affects us painfully; we can see its struggles and, sympathetically, feel something of its pain. The unseen agony of a plant leaves us indifferent. To a being with eyes a million times more sensitive than ours, the struggles of a dying plant would be visible and therefore distressing. Bose's instrument endows us with this more than microscopical acuteness of vision. The poisoned flower manifestly writhes before us. The last moments are so distressingly like those of a man, that we are shocked by the newly revealed spectacle of them into a hitherto unfelt sympathy.

Sensitive souls, whom a visit to the slaughter-house has converted to vegetarianism, will be well advised, if they do not want to have their menu still further reduced, to keep clear of the Bose Institute. After watching the murder of a plant, they will probably want to confine themselves to a strictly mineral diet. But the new self-denial would be as vain as the old. The ostrich, the sword swallower, the glass-eating fakir are as cannibalistic as the frequenters of chop-houses, take life as fatally as do the vegetarians. Bose's earlier researches on metals – researches which show that metals respond to stimuli, are subject to fatigue and react to poisons very much as living vegetable and animal organisms do – have deprived the conscientious practitioners of *ahimsa* of their last hope. They must be cannibals, for the simple reason that everything, including the 'inanimate,' is alive.

This last assertion may seem – such is the strength of inveterate prejudice – absurd and impossible. But a little thought is enough to show that it is, on the contrary, an assertion of what is *a priori* probable. Life exists. Even the most strict and puritanical physicists are compelled, albeit grudgingly, to admit the horridly disquieting fact. Life exists, manifestly, in a small part of the world we know. How did it get there? There are two possible answers. Either it was, at a given moment, suddenly introduced into a hitherto completely inanimate world from outside and by a kind of miracle. Or else it was, with consciousness, inherent in the ultimate particles of matter and, from being latent, gradually extrinsicated itself in ever-increasingly complicated and perfect forms. In the present state of knowledge – or ignorance, put it how you will – the second answer seems the more likely to be correct. If it is correct, then one might expect that inanimate matter would behave in the same way as does matter which is admittedly animate. Bose has shown that it does. It reacts to stimuli, it suffers fatigue, it can be killed. There is nothing in this that should astonish us. If the conclusion shocks our sense of fitness, that is only due to the fact that we have, through generations, made a habit of regarding matter as something dead; a lump that can be moved, and whose only real attribute is extension. Motion and extension are easily measured and can be subjected to mathematical treatment. Life, especially in its higher, conscious forms, cannot. To deny life to matter and concentrate only on its measurable qualities was a sound policy that paid by results. No wonder we made a habit of it. Habits easily become a part of us. We take them for granted, as we take for granted our hands and feet, the sun, falling downstairs instead of up, colours and sounds. To break a physical habit may be as painful as an amputation; to question the usefulness of an old-established habit of thought is felt to be an outrage, an indecency, a horrible sacrilege.

Crains dans le mur aveugle un regard qui t'épie.

It was all very well from a poet. One could smile indulgently at a pleasing and childish fancy. But when it came to laboratory experiments and graphs, things, it was felt, were getting more serious. It was time to make a protest.

Personally, I make no protest. Being only a literary man, and not one of those physicists whose professional interest it is to keep matter in its place, with only such attributes as render it amenable to mathematics, I am delighted. I love matter, I find it miraculous, and it pleases me when a serious man, like Bose, comes along and gives it a new certificate of merit.

In the philosophy books matter is generally spoken of slightingly, as something lumpish and crude. To the subtlety of their own minds, on the other hand, the metaphysicians can never pay a sufficiently glowing tribute. But in reality – if I may be pardoned the philosophically gross expression – it is to matter, not mind, that the attributes of subtlety, fineness, complexity belong. Our mental picture of the world and its component parts is a crude symbolical affair, having about as much relation to the original as a New Guinea idol to the human body. It is precisely because it is so crude and simple that the thought-picture is valuable to us. Reality – again I apologize – is infinitely too complicated for our understanding. We must simplify. But having simplified, we ought not to say that those Papuan images of the world, which are our philosophical and religious systems, our scientific hypotheses, are subtle; they are not. They are crude, compared with the original, and it is, precisely, their crudeness which gives them value, for us. Year by year our world-picture becomes increasingly complicated. More details are noted in the original and are incorporated, symbolically, into the image. If the mind of man develops and grows more subtle, that is due to the fact that each succeeding generation is brought up with a progressively more complete and elaborate thought-picture of the world and all its details. We think, we also feel, more subtly and multifariously than did the ancients. To our posterity, a thousand years from now, our subtleties will seem, no doubt, most barbarously crude. Perfection will be attained when mind has completely understood matter and is therefore as delicate, as complex, as variously rich as it. That is to say, perfection will never be attained.

On the Hoogly

The ship slides down the Hoogly, between the mudbanks and the palms. Every now and then we pass a village, a huge white jute mill. Above the flat plain of the delta the sky is enormous and peopled with majestic clouds. After these months lived under a perpetually flawless blue, the spectacle of clouds is a delight and a refreshment. I understand, now, the inspiration of those Mogul paintings, which represent princesses and great lords looking at the clouds. A dry season in India makes one long for a break in the monotony of too perfect weather. Cloud-gazing, when at last the approaching rains render it possible, must be a most delicious pastime, particularly when combined (as the Moguls in the paintings combine it) with dalliance, the sipping of sherbet, and the slow deliberate smoking of an enormous hubble-bubble.

These clouds are messengers from the world that lies beyond the borders of India; my pleasure at seeing them is symbolical. For, to tell the truth, I am glad to be leaving India. I have met old friends in India, and made new friends; I have seen many delightful and interesting things, much beauty, much that is strange, much that is grotesque and comical. But all the same I am glad to be going away. The reasons are purely selfish. What the eye does not see, the heart does not grieve over. It is because I do not desire to grieve that I am glad to be going. For India is depressing as no other country I have ever known. One breathes in it, not air, but dust and hopelessness. The present is unsatisfactory, the future dubious and menacing. The forces of the West have been in occupation for upwards of a century and a half. And yet five generations of peace and settled government have made the country, as a whole, no more prosperous than it was in the days of anarchy; according to some authorities, such as Digby, they have made it much poorer. Millions, at any rate, are still admittedly without enough to eat, all their lives. Custom and ancient superstition are still almost as strong as they ever were, and after a century and a half of Western government, nine Indians out of ten cannot read or write, and the tenth, who can, detests the Europeans who taught him. The educated and politically conscious profess democratic principles; but their instincts are profoundly and almost ineradicably aristocratic. They desire, theoretically, to see the country 'progressing' in the Western sense of the term; but the practical ambition of most of them is to secure a quiet job without responsibilities or risks.

Meanwhile the mountains of unnecessary labour, of inevitable hardship and superfluous suffering, are piled up, patiently, higher and ever higher. Millions upon millions are born and painfully live – to what end? God knows, it is hard enough to find a reason anywhere, West or East. But in India there is no conceivable answer to the question, at any rate in terms of the present existence. Metempsychosis had to be invented, and the doctrine of *karma* elaborated with a frightful logic, before the serried, innumerable miseries of India could be satisfactorily accounted for.

The ship goes sliding down-stream. The clouds seem to beckon and lead on, away. To-morrow we shall be at sea.

Rangoon

The precincts of the Shwe Dagon pagoda contain the world's finest specimens of what I may call the merry-go-round style of architecture and decoration. The huge bell-shaped spire, gilded from top to bottom and shining, towards the sun, with intolerable high lights, stands in the midst; and round it are grouped the hundreds of subsidiary shrines, elaborately fretted, glittering like Aladdin's cave at the pantomime with a gaudy mosaic of coloured glass, gilded and painted, or dark, with the natural colour of the teakwood pinnacles and gables, against the golden shining of the pagoda. It seems a sacred Fun Fair, a Luna Park dedicated to the greater glory of Gautama – but more fantastic, more wildly amusing than any Bank Holiday invention. Our memories, after a first visit, were of something so curiously improbable, so deliriously and comically dream-like, that we felt constrained to return the following day to make quite sure that we had really seen it.

On the Irrawaddy

Ancient geographers imagined a river running completely round the earth. Travelling up the Irrawaddy from Mandalay, I wished that their fancy had been the truth. How delightful it would have been to go on and on in that leisured and comfortable paddle-steamer, gliding calmly through every temperature and nation, every city of the earth, and every natural phenomenon! The banks slide past, the country opens and shuts like a fan, plays the peacock with its plains and avenues and receding dykes. Turning deliberately, the mountains exhibit, now one face, now another, now a garment of sunset rose, now of black against the stars, now of green, now of dim remote indigo and purple. From time to time cities and villages variously beckon. On jutting headlands the stumps of ancient towers and temples look down and consider the reflection of their irrevocably perished splendour. And all the time the current symbolically flows, the sailing ships, the rafts, the little canoes approach, drift past, recede and vanish like so many lives and loves. Such is river travelling at its best, as it ought to be – as it certainly would be, if the ancient geographers were right and the earth were indeed girdled by a cosmic stream.

The upper reaches of the Irrawaddy would certainly form a section of this great imaginary river. In their kind they are perfect. Between Mandalay and Bhamo I found myself constantly reminded of those strange and beautiful pages in which Edgar Allan Poe describes 'The Domain of Arnheim.' It is long years since I read the story; but I remember vividly the crystal river which gave access to the domain, I remember the white sands, the green and sloping lawns, the flowering trees, the woods – all the natural beauties so artfully arranged. For the domain of Arnheim was a masterpiece in the art of landscape gardening; it was nature, but composed; it was the non human chaos of the world informed by the spirit of man. The hills and jungles of Upper Burma are savagely innocent of human arrangement; but chance has often contrived to group them significantly and with art about their central river. Here, on a certain calm evening, the water and the plain, the distant mountains, the limpid greenish sky fell all at once into ready-made Claude Lorraines; and the white pagoda in the foreground, on the river's bank, was a fragment of ancient Rome, a ruin of Carthage. Claude persisted for miles; and appropriately enough, while we were steaming through him, a cool delicious fragrance, like the scent of distant tobacco flowers, haunted the air. It seemed as though the spirit of his art were finding expression in terms of another sense than that of sight.

At another place the hills came nearer; the narrow strip of plain between the river and their feet was covered with teak trees, intensely and darkly green. It was late afternoon; the trees shone in the warm and level light, the hills behind them were flushed, and at a certain moment the vision framed in the open window was a strong and glowing Constable. And in the defiles, where the river breaks through a range of hills and the thick multitudinous jungle comes swarming down to the water's edge, each turn of the stream revealed a rich fantastic composition – the composition of some artist not yet born, but destined, it was obvious, to be a master.

But not every landscape is a work of art, and river travelling is not invariably delightful. So, alas, we discovered, as we journeyed down-stream from Mandalay towards Rangoon. The weather, as we advanced, grew almost hourly more oppressive; the cattle and hides with which our steamer was loaded, piercingly stank; the landscape was almost as poor as the food. On either side of the mile-wide river the country was mostly flat and treeless. For a day we steamed through the pale and arid hills of the Burma oil-fields. An immense black smoke, visible through all a morning's navigation, streamed half across the sky. A strike was in progress; the Burmese, who objected, justifiably from all accounts, to the Wild West methods and cinema manners of the American drillers, had committed a murder and set a light to eight hundred thousand gallons of petroleum. A spirited race, the Burmese – a little too highly so, perhaps. But whatever the rights and wrongs, in these particular circumstances, of murder and arson, that streamer of black smoke certainly did something to enliven the prospect. I regretted it when at last it sank out of sight.

But the monotony was not entirely without alleviations. At

Pakkoku, for example (Pakkoku, which the French lady on the steamer would insist on calling 'Pas Cocu' – I suppose because her husband so manifestly was one), an acrobat was doing extraordinary things on a slack rope. At another town, whose less significant name I have forgotten, we stopped for several hours to embark some scores of tons of monkey-nuts. They were bound for Rangoon, and thence, I learned, for Marseilles, where, in due course, they would be turned into Pure Superfine Provençal Olive Oil. At a village lower down the river, we shipped the best part of a thousand lacquered kettle-drums – for home consumption, I suppose. They were charming instruments, shaped like enormous egg-cups – a foot, a stalk, a bowl with the parchment stretched across its mouth. What a cargo of potential Burmese happiness we were carrying under those taut diaphragms! But none leaked out into the ship. It was an odious voyage, and when at last we reached Prome, whence the railway starts for Rangoon, it was with a feeling of profound relief that we disembarked. Near the landing-stage stood two tall trees, sparse-leaved against the sky, and laden with an innumerable and repulsive fruitage of sleeping bats. The sun was sinking. With the waning of the light the bats began to stir. What had seemed a vegetable unfolded, and slowly stretched a leathery wing. There was a sudden flutter, an agitation of twigs, and two of the pendulous black fruits came together and began to make love, head downwards.

Bhamo

Between the main street of Bhamo and the river-bank, or what will be the river-bank, after the rains – for at this dry season the water is distant a hundred yards or more across a beach of sand – lies a little plain of two or three acres. It is a much trodden, dusty plat of land and, save for one enormous tree growing in the midst, quite bare. It is a fine tree, not at all tropical in aspect, but oak-like, with long limbs, branching almost horizontally from the trunk some fifteen or twenty feet above the ground. The very image of those great trees which, in Callot's etchings, give shelter to the encamped gypsies, protect the archers, as they do their target practice on St Sebastian, from the rays of the sun, or serve as convenient gallows for the victims of war. But it was not alone the tree that reminded me of Callot; it was its setting, it was the whole scene. The river in its mile-wide bed, with the flat fields beyond it, provided for the solitary tree that background of blank interminable extension, to which Callot was always so partial. Nor was the bustle immediately beneath and around the tree less characteristic than the blank behind it. Horses and little mules stood tethered beside their loaded pack-saddles. Men came and went with burdens, or stood in groups round one of the patient beasts. In the foreground food was being cooked over a fire and, squatting on their heels, other men were eating. Under the huge tree and against the blank background of receding flatness and empty sky, a multitudinous and ant-like life was being busily lived. It might have been the break-up of a gypsy encampment, or the tail end of Impruneta Fair, or a military bivouac out of the *Miseries of War*. It might have been – but in fact it was the starting of one of the caravans that march, laden with cotton and Burmese silk, Burmese jade and rubies, over the hills into China.

Bhamo

Lying as it does but thirty miles from the Chinese frontier, Bhamo is more than half a Chinese town. On its northern fringes stands a sizeable joss-house. The Chinese resort there to pray, to burn candles and incense, to record their wishes, and to discover by the religious equivalent of tossing – heads or tails – whether the gods have consented to their fulfilment. They go there also to drink tea and gamble, even to smoke a quiet pipe of opium. One spectral creature, at any rate, was doing so when we walked through the temple. Near him a group of his fellows were busily dicing; blank-eyed, ivory-faced, he sat apart, remote, as though he were inhabiting, as indeed he was, another world.

The inner courts, the actual shrine of the joss-house, were extravagant in their chinoiserie. Those fretted roofs, those great eaves turning up at the corners like horns, those tall thin pillars, those golds and scarlets, those twilights peopled by gilded images, serene or grotesque – all these things, one felt, might almost have been designed by Lady Orford, they seemed almost the *dix-huitième* parody of Chinese art. Fantastic they were, eminently amusing, even good in their way; only the way happened to be rather a tiresome one. But if, within, the joss-house was a Manchu extravagance, without it achieved the simple and supremely elegant beauty of an earlier period. The gate-house of the temple was a small white stuccoed building, quite plain except for the raised panels of brickwork which strengthened the angles of the façade and, like the ornamental pilasters of our classical architecture, served to underline the vertical movement of the design. It was covered with a low tiled roof, discreetly turned up at the corners, that the dead horizontal line might be made supple and alive. At the bottom, in the centre, one of those circular gateways, to which the Chinese are so partial, gave access to the inner courts of the temple. Above and to either side of it a pair of square windows lighted the upper floor. And that was all. But the proportions were so perfect, the gate and the windows so rightly placed, the faintly curving roof so graceful, that the little building seemed a masterpiece. Its simple and assured elegance made me think of Italy – of little stucco pavilions on the Brenta, of Tuscan and Roman villas, of all those unpretentious yet beautiful, yet truly noble houses which adorn the Italian countryside. This Chinese gate-house was classical, the product of an ancient and traditional art, slowly perfected. Here in Burma, where the national architecture is the architecture of the travelling circus and the amusement park, it seemed doubly beautiful. And when we went out into the streets, we found the same perfected and classical beauty for sale at every Chinese shop at two or three annas a specimen. The little Chinese tea-cups of earthenware, glazed white within, bird's-egg green without, are the cheapest crockery, and among the most beautiful, in the world. The Chinese shopkeepers were all but giving them away. And the bowls like eight-petalled flowers, painted with cocks and roses, yellow and pale vermilion and green on a softly glazed white ground – how much were we asked for those? I forget; but it was certainly well under sixpence apiece. Their beauty was worth a little fortune.

We spent a shilling and walked back to the steamer, loaded with the lovely product of centuries of human patience, skill, and genius. In our cabin we unpacked our shillingsworth of Chinese civilization and examined it at leisure: it was overwhelmingly impressive.

On the Irrawaddy

My reading on the Irrawaddy was *The Glass Palace Chronicle of the Kings of Burma*. This curious work was prepared in 1829 at the command of King Bagyidaw, who appointed a committee of the most famous scholars to compile a definitive and authoritative chronicle from the existing records. The result is probably the most learned edition of a fairy tale that has ever been published.

The Burmese fancy has a peculiar flavour of its own. In the reigns of the good kings, for example, there were repeated showers of gems, a phenomenon of which I do not remember to have read in the fabulous history of any other people. And what remarkable things happened whenever a king died! Sometimes it was merely a matter of smoke issuing from the palace. But it was seldom that the country got off so lightly; a royal death ordinarily produced effects of a much more disturbing character. Planets and even the Pleiades would pass across the disk of the moon, or remain stationary for as much as seven months at a stretch. Sometimes the river would flow up country and light would stream from the earth. Sometimes – a mystery which the translator does not condescend to explain – the *deinnatthè* coincided with the *thingyan*. But perhaps the most unpleasant incident of all occurred when King Hkanlat died. 'About the time of his death an ogre wandered laughing over the whole country for full seven days; and the people who heard the ogre's laugh durst not sleep.' Long live the King; the Burmese must have repeated the loyal formula with a special and peculiar fervour.

This random selection of incidents from Burmese history is sufficient, I think, to indicate the character of the chronicle as a whole. It is a collection of fabulous anecdotes. But the charm of the fabulous quickly palls, and it would be impossible to read more than a very few pages of the *Glass Palace Chronicle*, if it were not for the solemn absurdities introduced into it by the compiling scholars. These learned men collated the several sources of their chronicle with the most laudable industry; they weighed the credibility of varying texts; they applied the principles of Higher Criticism to the ancient records and were bold to reject even that which was old, if it offended against reason and authoritative tradition. How learnedly and with what sober criticism do they deal, for example, with the story of the Naga princess who had an affair with the Sun Prince and, in consequence, laid a number of eggs which hatched out, some into human children and some, surprisingly, into iron and rubies! The comments of the scholars are too long and too intricately learned to be quoted in full. But this is how they deal with the question of the Naga princess's eggs: –

'As for the statement that a human being was born from the union of the Sun Prince and a female Naga, these are the only parallel instances in the books: in the *Bhuridatta Jataka*, the birth of a human being after the father's kind from the union of a human prince with a female Naga and the birth of a Naga after the father's kind from the union of Dhattharattha, the Naga King, with the Princess Samuddaja; and in the *Mahavamsa*, such tales as the birth of Prince Sihabahu after the mother's kind from the union of the human princess, daughter of King Vangaraja, with a lion. Even if there were real union between the Sun Prince and the female Naga, either a spirit or a Naga should have been born, after the kind either of the father or the mother. Therefore, that a human son was born and not a spirit, nor a Naga, is contrary to reason, and this is a point of variance with the books.

'As for the statement that one golden egg broke in the land of Mogok Kyappyin and became stone, iron and ruby, this land of Mogok Kyappyin being thus singled out from among the fifty-six places of precious stones on the surface of Jambadapa, it is worth considering whether, in other places also, the various kinds of gems, stones, iron, ruby, gold and silver, and pearl, were likewise the result of the breaking of a Naga egg. Not a shadow, not a hint,' the scholars vehemently conclude, 'appears in the books that in all these fifty-six places a Naga egg broke and became stone, iron, or ruby.'

It is crushing, it is utterly conclusive. The female Naga and all her eggs must be rejected. Reason and authority demand that we should accept a more probable account of the origin of the young Pyusawhti, the Prince who killed, with a magic bow, the Great Boar, the Great Bird, the Giant Tiger and the Monstrous Flying Squirrel.

It is as though a committee of Scaligers and Bentleys had assembled to edit the tales of the nursery. Perrault's chronicle of Red

Riding Hood is collated with Grimm's, the variants recorded, the credibility of the two several versions discussed. And when that little matter has been satisfactorily dealt with, there follows a long and incredibly learned discussion of the obscure, the complex and difficult problems raised by Puss in Boots. What language did the cat talk? And was he black or tortoise-shell, ginger or common tabby? Scaliger inclines to Latin and tortoise-shell. Bentley, with more weight of evidence, prefers black and Hebrew. A pleasing fancy. But when we pass from Red Riding Hood and Puss in Boots to the fables of the Old Testament, the fancy becomes a fact. In America, it would appear, there are still people who can discuss the first chapter of Genesis, the stories of Noah and Joshua, with all the earnest gravity of Burmese pandits discussing the Sun Prince and the eggs of the female Naga.

PART TWO
Malaya

Penang

Penang has a certain Sicilian air. It is a sort of Palermo, lacking indeed the architecture and the orange groves, those characteristically Mediterranean amenities, but rich in a tropical wealth of wicker huts and naked children, of coco palms and jungle. Walking on the Peak, we found ourselves at a certain point looking down an almost precipitous ravine into the forest. We were in a fold of the hills, shut off from the sea breeze. It was prodigiously hot, and from the dense green tangle below us there came up a thick and hardly breathable steam, that smelt like that first hot and sweetish puff of air which fills your nostrils and condenses in blinding moisture on your spectacles, as you open the door of the Great Palm House at Kew Gardens. There could be no mistake this time; we were genuinely in the tropics.

Penang

We were in Penang on the last day of the Chinese New Year celebrations. The temples were thronged with a crowd mostly of women and young girls. They were exquisitely and richly dressed. Gold pins and flowers were stuck in their glossy black hair. Their earrings and bracelets were of the translucent jade which commands among the Celestials a price that seems to us fantastic.

And what beauty, what a charm they had! From the smooth ivory faces the bright and, for us at any rate, strangely expressionless eyes looked out, startlingly black against the pale skin. The lovely and perverse creatures who float through Marie Laurencin's paintings have the same smooth whiteness of cheek and forehead, the same black, bright and bird-like regard. And the long slender Chinese necks – these too were Laurencinian. And the exquisite fine hands. But Marie Laurencin's beauties have a length of leg and a grace of movement in which these charming Celestials were sadly lacking. Chinese hands are generally beautiful, and the gestures that are made with them have a wonderful refinement, a traditional and artistic elegance. But the walk of the Chinese woman is curiously without grace. It is a toddle, charming and appealing in its absurdity, but totally without dignity. Their hands move classically and in the Grand Manner; but their walk is trivially rococo. They are, so to speak, High Renaissance from the waist upwards and a Louis Philippe bibelot below. The imperial deportment of the Indian women seems to be quite unknown among the Chinese. But then the Indians, like the peasant women of Italy, who bear themselves like queens, are accustomed to carrying burdens on their heads. The Chinese, as far as I know, are not. Nothing so much improves the deportment as the balancing of a six gallon jar on the crown of the skull. There are plenty of European as well as Chinese ladies whose appearance would be vastly improved by a daily performance of this exercise. It would as effectively correct the Western droop and slouch as the Extreme Oriental toddle.

Between Penang and Singapore

Our journey from Penang to Singapore began at night. We were carried in darkness through the invisible forest. The noise of the insects among the trees was like an escape of steam. It pierced the roaring of the train as a needle might pierce butter. I had thought man pre-eminent at least in the art of noise-making. But a thousand equatorial cicadas could shout down a steel works; and with reinforcements they would be a match for machine-guns.

Morning revealed the forest, hushed now under the light. The railway line was a little groove, scored through the growing layers of green down to the red earth. Fifty yards to either side of the train rose the walls of the cutting. Looking at them I wondered where in this solid verdure the uproarious insects found a place to live.

Every tourist is haunted by the desire to 'get off the Beaten Track.' He wants, in the first place, to do something which other people have not done. The longing to be in some way or other unique grows with every increase of standardization. American advertisers, whom it pays to be psychologists, have understood this pathetic trait in the character of their contemporaries. In what are, for some reason, styled the 'Better Magazines' you will see dignified advertisements of motor-cars, overcoats, radio sets, note-paper, chocolates, whose outstanding merit is announced to be their 'exclusiveness.' The word attracts a million buyers, who cherish their mass-produced treasure as though it were a masterpiece, and who feel proud – at any rate until they meet a few of their fellow- buyers – in the 'exclusive' possession of something unique. The tourist is like the reader of advertisements. He wants something for his money which nobody else possesses. Everybody has been to Rome; but few have visited Nepi. Java is well known; but who has landed at Ternate or Lombok? It is delightful to be able to get up in a Western drawing-room and say: 'When I was last in the interior of Papua . . .'

But it is not alone the desire to achieve uniqueness that makes the tourist so anxious to leave the Beaten Track. It is not the anticipated pleasure of boasting about his achievements. The incorrigible romantic in every one of us believes, with a faith that is proof against all disappointments, that there is always something more remark-able off the Beaten Track than on it, that the things which it is difficult and troublesome to see must for that very reason be most worth seeing. Those who travel pursue some phantom which perpetually eludes them; they are always hoping to discover some mode of life that is somehow fundamentally different from any mode with which they are familiar; and they imagine that they will be able, magically, as soon as they have found it, to get into contact with this marvellous existence, to understand and partake in it. In the obvious places and on the Beaten Track, they never find what they are looking for. On the Beaten Track, through whatever part of the world it may lead, men and women live always in very much the same way, and there is no Open Sesame to their intimacy. But perhaps off the Beaten Track, in the little out-of-the-way places, where the hotels are bad and there are toads in the bathroom – perhaps where there are no hotels, but only rest-houses, with centipedes – perhaps in the places where you must bring your own tents and porters, with provisions and ammunition for a campaign of weeks – perhaps where there is nothing but the jungle and leeches, serpents and precipices and vampires and an occasional pygmy with a blowpipe and poisoned arrows . . . Perhaps. But even amongst the crocodiles and the cannibals the secret still eludes you. Life is still fundamentally the same. Men and women are as difficult to know as ever – rather more so, on the whole; for your knowledge of Pygmy is rudimentary and the little people are afraid.

It was with such meditations that I allayed the desire to leave the Beaten Track, which the spectacle of the jungle had evoked in me. To be devoured by leeches in the pursuit of something as hopelessly unattainable as the foot of the rainbow – was it worth it? Obviously not. And I thanked heaven and the British Empire for the F.M.S. railway. Still, I went on longing to get behind that wall of green; I went on longing, in the teeth of my own denials, that there was something miraculous and extraordinary in the other side. Meanwhile the train steamed on towards Singapore; an attendant from the restaurant car came in to tell us that breakfast was ready.

A little later my longings were cured, for the time being at any rate, by the disappearance of that which had aroused them. The jungle suddenly vanished and its place was taken by interminable rubber plantations. Even in maturity a rubber plantation is a poor thing. In youth it is an eyesore. Miserably scraggy little trees planted neatly in rows flanked the railway and continued to flank it during almost all the rest of the day. We rolled through literally hundreds of miles of potential Dunlops, of latent golf balls, and hot-water bottles to be. I own no rubber shares and am a consumer of tyres and crêpe soles. While admiring the energy of those who have destroyed it, I regretted the jungle. Here and there the train passed through a stretch of country that had ceased to be jungle and had not yet become plantation. The forest has been burnt. A great tract of brown desolation stretches away from the railway. The dead stumps of trees still stand, the charred trunks lie along the ground – the corpses and skeletons of a forest. Soon they will have been rooted out and dragged away. The Brazilian seedlings will be planted and in 1932 or thereabouts another million of goloshes and Malthusian squirts will be distributed throughout a grateful world.

Singapore

Cleared of the forests, tamed into park and garden, this tropical land seems, under its perennially clouded skies, a piece of temperate Europe. From our windows we looked out on to sloping lawns, set here and there with huge umbrageous trees that looked almost like elms and oaks. The clouds swam indolently overhead. A thin haze stippled the distances and made them tenderly dim. We might have been looking out over a park in the Thames valley, but a Thames valley, as you saw at a second glance, deliriously dreaming of palm trees and orchids, and where the air was as warm as blood. It was into an equatorial England that we had suddenly stepped.

Batavia, Java

Near the Penang Gate lies an old brass cannon, half buried in the mud. It has no history, it is quite unornamental. A more common-place piece of ordnance never issued from an eighteenth-century arsenal. The world is full of such old brass cannons. By all the rules it should have been melted down long ago or stuck muzzle downwards into the ground to serve as a post, or mounted on a little wooden carriage and left in the weather outside the door of a museum. But destiny decreed otherwise. Instead of suffering any of the ignominies usually reserved for its kind, this superannuated popgun was turned into a god. It lies there in the mud, wreathed with gardenias and orchids and a whole conservatory of paper flowers. The ground all about it is planted with long-stemmed paper lanterns, and incense burns perpetually before its muzzle. Two or three hawkers are encamped all day beside it, under the trees, like the sellers of books and plaster saints and candles in the shadow of a cathedral. The gun god's worshippers are numerous; they do a roaring trade in offerings and souvenirs. Great is the Cannon of the Batavians.

The Javanese were once Hindus, as their neighbours of Bali are to this day. But now, with the other Malayan peoples of Sumatra and the peninsula, they are Mohammedans. Mohammedans in name, at any rate; for their monotheism is hardly more than a varnish spread over cults much more ancient and, in the tropical circumstances, much more apposite. Pure monotheism is probably the last religion that would suggest itself to the minds of men living near the equator. In a tropical jungle, only a blind deaf-mute could be a monotheist. The woods are horrible; they teem with countless small and separate mysteries – unaccountable sights in the half-darkness, inexplicable sounds across the silence. Nobody with ears and eyes could fail, in a jungle, to be a believer in spirits, ghosts and devils. The Malays may call themselves Moslems; but they are still, at heart and by nature, animists.

Nor is it to the spirits alone that they pay their devotions. There is no God but God and Mohammed is his prophet. No doubt. But a cannon is cylindrical and, long before they became Moslems, the Javanese were worshippers of the reproductive principle in nature. An immemorial phallism has crystallized round the old gun, transforming it from a mere brass tube into a potent deity, to be propitiated with flowers and little lanterns, to be asked favours of with smoking incense. Men come and, standing before the sacred symbol, silently implore assistance. Women desirous of offspring sit on the prostrate God, rub themselves against his verdigrised sides and pray to him for increase. Even white ladies, it is said, may be seen at evening alighting inconspicuously from their motor-cars at the Penang Gate. They hurry across the grass to where the God is lying. They drop a few gardenias and a supplication, they touch the God's unresponsive muzzle; then hurry back again through the twilight, fearful of being recognized, of being caught in the flagrant act of worshipping at the shrine of a God who was being adored a thousand generations before Adam was ever thought of and beside whom the Gods of Zoroaster and the Vedas, of Moses and Christ and Mohammed are the merest upstarts and parvenus.

Batavia

'In matters of commerce,' it was once affirmed,

> 'In matters of commerce the fault of the Dutch
> Is giving too little and asking too much.'

But either things have changed since those lines were written, or else the Dutch do not regard the selling of food as commerce. For there are restaurants in Holland where, for a remarkably reasonable price, one may eat, not only much more, but also much better food than can be had anywhere else in the world. The five-shilling luncheon at the Restaurant Royal at the Hague is at once Gargantuan and delicious. For a foreigner, not yet trained up to Dutch standards, the hors-d'oeuvre alone are satiatingly sufficient. By the time the sixth or seventh course has made its appearance, he throws up the fork and retires, leaving the inured Olympic athletes of the jaw and stomach in undisputed possession of the restaurant. For the hardiest of these heroes – and heroines – the proprietors of the Royal provide a luncheon at ten shillings; it must be almost time, when they have finished eating it, to go and dress for dinner.

My gastronomic experiences in Holland led me to expect a no less fabulous profusion in Colonial Java. But I was disappointed, or perhaps relieved, to find that the hotels catered not for giants but for men and women only about twice life size. The only truly Rabelaisian feature of Javanese diet is the Rice Table. The Rice Table must be seen, and eaten, to be believed. Without the co-operation of the gullet, faith cannot swallow it. I do not even expect those who have never eaten a Rice Table to believe my description. Marco Polo, when he returned from the court of the Great Khan, full of true stories and correct statistics, was by his compatriots derisively nicknamed 'Marco Milione.' For the sake of the truth about Rice Tables, I am prepared with old Mark Million to be thought a liar; here then it is – the truth, literal but unbelievable.

It is lunch time. You enter the dining-room of the hotel. A little old yellow waiter, looking less like a man than a kindly orang-utan,

shaved and with a batik handkerchief tied round its head, shows you
to your place, asks what you will eat. You push aside the menu of the
commonplace European lunch.

'Ane Rice Tafel for mich,' you say, combining German and
Lowland Scotch into what you believe, quite erroneously, to be the
language of Holland. The kindly little monkey-man trots off,
smiling; it seems to please him when his clients decide on the Rice
Table. You wait. In a little while the monkey-man's embassy to the
kitchen has its effect. A waiter appears at your elbow with an
enormous cauldron of rice; you heap your plate with it. He moves
away. Immediately another waiter takes his place, offering fish soup.
You damp your rice; the soup man goes. A dish of chops at once
replaces the tureen. Looking round, you see that the chop carrier is
standing at the head of a long procession of Javanese waiters,
extending in unbroken line from your table right across the dining-
room to the kitchen door. Each time you help yourself, the procession advances a step and a new dish is presented. I took the trouble
one day to count the number of dishes offered me. Twenty-six
actually appeared before me; but it was a busy day for the waiters
and I do not think I got all the dishes I was entitled to. They
included after the chops, two other kinds of meat, two kinds of bird,
a species of sausage; fish, both fresh and dried; roast bananas;
several kinds of vegetables, plain and curried; two varieties of salads;
fried nuts, numerous pickles; jam, a queer kind of unleavened bread,
and various other things which I cannot at the moment remember.
All these articles are thoroughly stirred in with the rice on your plate
– a trough would be a more suitable receptacle – the napkin is
tucked firmly into place beneath the chin, and leaning forward you
shovel the immense and steaming mound of food down your throat.

But the Rice Table is really the only inordinate feature of Dutch
East Indian diet. The breakfast table may be furnished with such
ill-timed delicacies as Edam cheese, gingerbread and liver sausage;
but the porridge, the cooked meats, the eggs and fishes, the toast, the
scones and marmalade of the Anglo-Saxon breakfast are lacking.
Afternoon tea is strictly tea; one drinks, but one does not eat. Dinner
is perfectly normal and late supper is unknown. Hotels within the
British Empire may be innocent of the Rice Table; but the total
amount of nourishment which they offer in the course of each day,

and which is consumed by their clients, is decidedly greater than
that which forms the daily foundation of Greater Holland. With the
possible exception of the Americans, the English are, I am afraid,
the world's heaviest eaters. They call us in Italy 'il popolo dei cinque
pasti' – the Five Meal People.

Frenchmen and Italians eat normally a little more than half the
amount of food consumed by prosperous Englishmen. Arabs and
Indians about a third or a quarter. Seeing that mental and bodily
efficiency can be attained and kept up on these smaller quantities, it
follows that at least half our eating is a matter, not of hunger or
need, but of pure gluttony, of simple and uncontrolled hoggishness.

Gluttony is numbered among the Seven Deadly Sins; but for some
reason – perhaps because it is now so universally practised in
respectable society – the sin is seldom denounced. Lasciviousness is
deplored by every one; anger with its attendant violences, by a
majority, at any rate in the Western and democratic countries. But
gluttony, the besetting vice of our age – for never in the world's
history have so many men and women eaten so immoderately as
they do now – gluttony goes almost unreproved. In the Middle Ages
on the other hand, when food was scarce and over-eating singular
and conspicuous, gluttony was freely denounced. Peace, prosperity,
the colonization of new lands, refrigerators, easy transport and
modern agriculture have made food plentiful, at any rate in the
West. Gluttony being universal is scarcely noticed, and all the fury
of the moralists is spent on other sins, especially lasciviousness.

Now the gravity of a sin is gauged by several standards, which we
employ, when we make our judgements, either separately or
together. We may judge a sin, in the first place, by the degree of its
harmfulness to the society in which the sinner lives. Thus, the sin of
anger, when it leads to crimes of violence, is harmful to the society in
which the angry man lives, and therefore grave. Avarice is chiefly
detested because it leads to theft and dishonest practices, which do
mischief to the avaricious man's neighbours. And so on. The
application to each particular sin is easily made.

But sin is not exclusively a social matter; its gravity is also
measured by the harm, mental or physical (and the physical is
always finally also a mental mischief), it does to the sinner himself.
The first and axiomatic duty of a man is, I suppose, to make the best

use he can of such talents as he possesses, to develop his latent powers and keep himself at the highest pitch of efficiency. His first duty, in a word, is to be himself. The majority of human beings live in conditions which make it impossible for them to be themselves. A slum is, so to speak, an Original Sin common to all its inhabitants and for which they are not individually responsible. But a substantial minority of men and women cannot plead the Original Sin of bad conditions to excuse their failure to be fully themselves. These are personally accountable. For to bury talents, to frustrate development of one's own powers, to compromise the efficiency of mind or body are sins. It is for this reason, rather than because they do harm to others beside the sinner, that the various forms of sloth, lust, intemperance and self-complacent pride are sinful.

Historical circumstances may cause the gravity of sins to change at different epochs. Thus, in a warlike society, whose very existence depends on the courage and ferocity of the individuals composing it, the sin of anger will not be a grave one; nor will the crimes of violence which accompany it be considered worthy of severe censure. Our Saxon fathers could kill a man for a few shillings; the punishment fitted the crime and was proportionate, at that period, to the sin. Later in the history of Western Europe there was a definite moment at which lasciviousness became a much graver sin than it had hitherto been. Before the introduction of venereal diseases, a moderate lechery might do a certain but not very serious mischief to society; but it did very little harm, either spiritually or physically, to the lecher. Innocent of disease, a temperately lascivious Greek was almost innocent of sin. The Christians, as innocent at first of disease, artificially invested the instinct with an aura of personal and social sinfulness. Later, when the Crusaders returned with their deplorable souvenirs of Oriental travel, pleasure really and indeed became a crime. A single lapse, not a course of excesses, could reduce a man to repulsive disfigurement, madness, paralysis and death. Nor did he suffer alone; he murdered his wife as well as himself and condemned his children to blindness, deafness and deformity. Mercury and arsenic have done much to diminish the personal sinfulness of a moderate lechery. Its social sinfulness is succumbing to divorce and contraception, is dwindling with the gradual decay of Christian intolerance. The progress of medicine and common sense may end by making us as innocent as were the ancient Greeks.

It was, as I have already pointed out, a combination of historical circumstances – a combination of industrial prosperity with colonization and imperialism, of scientific agriculture with steam transport – that made our modern gluttony possible. It escapes censure, in our English-speaking countries, at any rate, because its evil effects upon society are not immediately manifest, like those of avarice or anger, and because it does not so immediately take its toll from the individual as does excessive lechery or the intemperate use of drugs. But though not immediately manifest, the effects of gluttony are none the less deplorable. A large proportion of every man's available energy, mental and physical (it is the same), is exhausted in the process of an interminable and unnecessary digestion. More or less chronic costiveness reduces vitality by sending a stream of putrefactive poison circulating through the blood. The body is bloated with venom, the mind darkened by the glooms and uncharitablenesses that are the spiritual fruits of constipation. Suffering, the glutton causes his neighbours to suffer. And after forty or fifty years of gormandizing, a cancer makes its appearance and the victim of gluttony bids a long and excruciating farewell to the scenes of his vice. It was syphilis that turned even moderate and occasional lechery into sin. Cancer, which leaves the savage and the frugal Oriental unscathed, but preys with ever-increasing fury on the overfed Westerner, is the last-paid wage, the parting gift of a life of gluttony.

Much in the life of man to which we now attach 'spiritual' and transcendental values, might and perhaps should be revalued in terms of hygiene. Starting from the axiom that it is a man's first duty to use all his powers to the best purpose, to be as completely as possible himself, we can re-interpret a great deal of morality and religion as rules of health for the attainment and keeping up of an ideal efficiency. Many sins, it is obvious, make a man physically unhealthy, and therefore incapable of doing or being his best – a burden to himself and a nuisance to his neighbours. It is unnecessary to labour the point. But vice compromises other modes of healthful existence besides the physical. Sin is visited by punishments more subtle than constipation, venereal disease and all their unpleasant spiritual concomitants. For example, there are certain human potentialities which can only be developed into actuality when the mind is in a state of quiet. For those who live in a state of agitation, certain kinds of serene and lasting happiness, certain intellectual and creative processes, are impossible. Now it is precisely the excessive indulgence of those natural proclivities called 'sins' that tends to keep the mind in agitation and prevent a man from realizing what are perhaps the most important potentialities of thought and happiness he holds within him. Sloth, avarice, lechery and anger are hygienically unsound; they dull the mind and trouble it, raise mud, so to speak, by stirring. Reasonable activity of a kind which it is possible to believe worth white, a controlled temper, a chastity not so excessive as to be harmful, a humility unpreoccupied with the trivial fears, desires, and hopes which fill the life of the vain and proud – these things are hygienically sound, because they make it possible for the man who practises them to realize the potentialities which, were his mind kept by vice in a state of agitated distraction, would perforce remain latent and for ever unactual.

Mysticism, which is the systematic cultivation of mental quietness, the deliberate and conscious pursuit of the serenest kind of happiness, may be most satisfactorily regarded as a rule of health. Mystics attribute their happiness and their creative powers to a union with God. The hypothesis is, to say the least, unnecessary. Atheists and epileptics have received inspirations which have never been attributed to the Holy Spirit. Every symptom of the trance, from the 'sense of presence' to total unconsciousness, can be produced artificially in the laboratory. The drug taker, the epileptic, the suddenly 'inspired' mathematician or artist, the experimental psychologist differ from the religious mystic only in their attitude towards the mystical experiences which they all equally share. Believing them to be divine, the religious mystic cultivates his experiences, makes use of them to bring him happiness and serenity. The others accept them as merely curious sensations, like giddiness or the hiccups, and do not attempt, therefore, to make a systematic use of their experiences in the conduct of their lives. In this they are wrong.

We are, I think, fairly safe in supposing that religious mystics do not in fact unite themselves with that impossible being, a God at once almighty and personal, limited and limitless. But that does not in any way detract from the value of mysticism as a way to perfect health. No man supposes that he is entering into direct communion with the deity when he does Swedish exercises or cleans his teeth. If we make a habit of Müller and Pepsodent, we do so because they keep us fit. It is for the same reason that we should make a habit of mysticism as well as of moral virtue. Leading a virtuous and reasonable life, practising the arts of meditation and recollection, we shall unbury all our hidden talents, shall attain in spite of circumstances to the happiness of serenity and integration, shall come, in a word, to be completely and perfectly ourselves.

Batavia

Hygiene is doubtless an excellent thing. But I begin to wonder, as I re-read the preceding section, why I should have found it necessary to insist on hygiene to the total exclusion of God. Temperament, I suppose, is partly accountable. But it is mainly an affair – as usual – of unreasoning prejudices, the fruit of mental habits acquired during childhood. Men who have had a certain kind of training can see divinity, or the possibility of it, everywhere. Those whose upbringing has been of a different kind spend their whole lives sterilizing and hermetically sealing their universe, so as to prevent any germ of godhead from entering and breeding dangerously within it. They demand that the cosmos shall be bacteriologically pure. No life; hygiene, but at all costs not a god. Considered dispassionately, this prejudice does not seem to me any more worthy of respect than its opposite. Indeed, it is probably much less respectable.

The fact that men have had stupid and obviously incorrect ideas about God does not justify us in trying to eliminate God from out of the universe. Men have had stupid and incorrect ideas on almost every subject that can be thought about. They have believed, for example, that the earth is flat and that the sun revolves round it. But we do not regard that as a valid reason for denying the existence of astronomy.

The belief that God is a person and that a real personal contact can be established between him and a human being is probably unfounded. We are persons ourselves, and we therefore tend to see all things in terms of personality. The uneducated man of average intelligence tends, quite naturally and as a matter of course, to interpret a thunderstorm in terms of human feelings. Science provides a different and more satisfactory interpretation. All contemporary Western men and women possess at least the rudiments of physical science and the scientific habit of mind as an inheritance; they have been brought up to think of nature in terms of impersonal law, not in terms of anthropomorphic passion. Not even the stupidest European or American now imagines that a thunderstorm is a manifestation of divine tantrums. But among peoples brought up in a different way, only thinkers of the highest genius can conceive of a thunderstorm as a purely impersonal happening. There is no well-established science of religion. The stupid Westerner has almost no educational advantages, when it comes to religious matters, over his savage and Oriental brothers. His natural instinct is to regard God as a person, and he has received no training that might cause him to modify his first spontaneous opinion as it has modified his natural, untutored opinion about thunderstorms. Among primitive peoples there arise occasionally men of scientific genius who know, intuitively, the truth about thunderstorms. Where God is concerned, we are all more or less primitives; only the greatest religious geniuses have any knowledge (and it is knowledge of a personal, intuitive, hardly communicable kind) of the truth about God. It is significant that Buddha, whom one feels to have been the most intellectually powerful of all the great religious leaders, should have rejected completely the idea of a personal God and gone beyond it. Two thousand five hundred years hence the majority of human beings may have arrived at the position reached by Gautama two thousand five hundred years ago. We like to speak of ourselves as 'moderns'; but in point of fact the vast majority of us are the most barbarously primitive of ancients.

Batavia

Indian servants are scarcely more than pieces of moving furniture. They have obliterated themselves, and nothing remains in your presence but a kind of abstract and unindividualized efficiency – or inefficiency, as the case may be. But in Burma and throughout Malaya, wherever the servants are Chinamen or Malays, you become aware that the machine which makes your bed or pulls your rickshaw or waits upon you at table is human and has no desire to suppress the fact. Its eye is critical; the expressions on its face are comments on your words and actions. And when you walk in the streets you have an uncomfortable feeling that you are being judged and condemned to an eternal derision. The European woman is generally unaware in India that the attendant machine is a man; the thing is reliably sexless. The Burman, the Chinaman, the Malay, who have no knowledge of caste and consider themselves the equals of any man or woman, give no such comfortable assurance of sexlessness. To discover humanity – and of the most 'human,' the all too human variety – in what you have been accustomed to regard as a labour-saving device is rather disquieting.

Batavia

At Weltevreden there is a plot of ground dedicated to the pleasures of the natives and called the Gambier Park. At the entrance gate you pay according to your nationality – Javanese five cents, foreign Orientals (Chinese or Arab) fifteen, and Europeans, half a gulden. We admitted the equitableness of the tariff – for in every tropical land the poorest people are always the inhabitants – shouldered the white man's burden to the tune of fifty cents apiece, and walked in. The thick, almost palpable darkness of a night overcast by tropical clouds was tempered by a few sparse arc-lamps and by the dim lanterns of mineral-water vendors. Their light was reflected from puddles; it had been raining. The night felt and smelt like a hothouse. It seemed strange to be walking in the open. Surely there was a glass roof just overhead, there were glass walls all round us. And where were the hot-water pipes?

The sound of drums and bamboo xylophones, that tinkled out the endless and incoherent music of a dripping tap, drew us across the grass. Under a bright light twenty or thirty Javanese young men and girls were gravely dancing. Nobody spoke. They went through their evolutions without a word. I was reminded of the noiseless coming and going of an aquarium, of the mute ecstasies of embracing octopuses, of submarine battles, ferocious but inaudible. It is a strangely silent people, the Javanese. Some merman, perhaps, from the soundless depths among the corals was the first colonist of the island. We stood for some time watching the dumb Tritons in their batik skirts or trousers, the voiceless but, I am afraid, far from respectable nereids. Then, since one easily tires of goldfish, we strolled away in search of livelier entertainment.

But mum was still the word. Fifty yards away we found an open-air picture show. A crowd, as fishily dumb as the young dancers, stood or squatted in front of an illuminated screen, across which there came and went, in an epileptic silence, the human fishes of a cinema drama. And what a drama! We arrived in time to see a man in what the lady novelists call 'faultless evening dress,' smashing a door with an axe, shooting several other men, and then embracing against her will a distressed female, also in evening dress. Meanwhile another man was hurrying from somewhere to somewhere else, in motor-cars that tumbled over precipices, in trains that villains contrived to send full tilt into rivers – in vain, however, for the hurrying young man always jumped off the doomed vehicles in the nick of time and immediately found another and still more rapid means of locomotion. We did not stay to witness the foregone conclusion; but it was sufficiently obvious that the man in the hurry would find an aeroplane which would duly crash on the roof of the house where the distressed female was being embraced against her will. He would rush in and be just in time to prevent the consummation of a long protracted rape. (I may add parenthetically that rape, on the cinema, is always providentially leisurely; the villain takes things so easily that heroes invariably have the time to drive in

Straight-Eights from Salt Lake City to New York before the virtuous resistance of the heroine can be overcome.) The villain would then be shot and the young man and distressed female would embrace, lengthily and with gusto, over his carcase.

The violent imbecilities of the story flickered in silence against the background of the equatorial night. In silence the Javanese looked on. What were they thinking? What were their private comments on this exhibition of Western civilization? I wondered. In North Africa, in India, I have also wondered. There are many races, skins of many shades; there are the colonies of many white nations, there are protectorates and mandated territories; there are nominally free countries that give 'concessions' – a great variety of political institutions and subject peoples. But there is only one Hollywood. Arabs and Melanesians, negroes and Indians, Malays and China-men – all see the same films. The crook drama at Tunis is the same as the crook drama at Madras. On the same evening, it may be, in Korea, in Sumatra, in the Sudan, they are looking at the same seven soulful reels of mother-love and adultery. The same fraudulent millionaires are swindling for the diversion of a Burmese audience in Mandalay, a Maori audience in New Zealand. Over the entire globe the producers of Hollywood are the missionaries and propagandists of white civilization. It is from the films alone that the untaught and untravelled member of a subject race can learn about the superior civilization which has conquered and is ruling him.

And what does he learn from the films? What is this famous civilization of the white men which Hollywood reveals? These are questions which one is almost ashamed to answer. The world into which the cinema introduces the subject peoples is a world of silliness and criminality. When its inhabitants are not stealing, murdering, swindling or attempting to commit rape (too slowly, as we have seen, to be often completely successful), they are being maudlin about babies or dear old homes, they are being fantastically and idiotically honourable in a manner calculated to bring the greatest possible discomfort to the greatest possible number of people, they are disporting themselves in marble halls, they are aimlessly dashing about the earth's surface in fast-moving vehicles. When they make money they do it only in the most discreditable, unproductive and socially mischievous way – by speculation. Their politics are matters exclusively of personal (generally amorous) intrigue. Their science is an affair of secret recipes for making money – recipes which are always getting stolen by villains no less anxious for cash than the scientific hero himself. Their religion is all cracker mottoes, white-haired clergymen, large-hearted mothers, hard, Bible-reading, puritanical fathers, and young girls who have taken the wrong turning and been betrayed (the rapes, thank goodness, are occasionally successful) kneeling with their illegitimate babies in front of crucifixes. As for their art – it consists in young men in overalls and large ties painting, in cock-lofts, feminine portraits worthy to figure on the covers of magazines. And their literature is the flatulent verbiage of the captions.

Such is the white man's world as revealed by the films, a world of crooks and half-wits, morons and sharpers. A crude, immature, childish world. A world without subtlety, without the smallest intellectual interests, innocent of art, letters, philosophy, science. A world where there are plenty of motors, telephones and automatic pistols, but in which there is no trace of such a thing as a modern idea. A world where men and women have instincts, desires and emotions, but no thoughts. A world, in brief, from which all that gives the modern West its power, its political and, I like patriotically to think, its spiritual superiority to the East, all that makes it a hemisphere which one is proud to have been born in and happy to return to, has been left out. To the subject races of the East and South, Hollywood proclaims us as a people of criminals and mentally defectives. It was better, surely, in the old days before the cinema was invented, when the white men's subjects were totally ignorant of the world in which their masters lived. It was possible for them, then, to believe that the white men's civilization was something great and marvellous – something even greater, perhaps, and more extraordinary than it really was. Hollywood has changed all that. It has scattered broadcast over the brown and black and yellow world a grotesquely garbled account of our civilization. It has published a journal of our activities, but heavily censored. The political and scientific articles, the reviews of books, the essays, the reports of learned societies have been cut out; there are blanks where the reproductions of the works of art should be. Nothing has been left but the police court news, the feuilleton, the reports of the divorce cases. White men complain that the attitude of the members of the coloured races is not so respectful as it was. Can one be astonished?

What astonishes me is that the attitude remains as respectful as it does. Standing in the midst of that silent crowd of Javanese picture fans, I was astonished, when the performance attained its culminating imbecility, that they did not all with one accord turn on us with hoots of derision, with mocking and murderous violence. I was astonished that they did not all rush in a body through the town crying 'Why should we be ruled any longer by imbeciles?' and murdering every white man they met. The drivelling nonsense that flickered there in the darkness, under the tropical clouds, was enough to justify any outburst. But fortunately for us, the Oriental is patient and long-suffering. He is also cautious; for he knows, in the words of Hilaire Belloc, that

> Whatever happens, we have got
> The Maxim gun, and they have not——

'we' being the whites.

Maxim guns can check actions, but they cannot control thoughts. The coloured peoples think a great deal less of us than they did, even though they may be too cautious to act on their opinions. For this state of affairs the movies are not, of course, alone responsible. The spread of native education, the unedifying spectacle of the World War, the talk about self-determination and the sacredness of nationality, with promises of liberation made and never carried into effect – these have done much, perhaps most. But the share of Hollywood in lowering the white man's prestige is by no means inconsiderable. A people whose own propagandists proclaim it to be mentally and morally deficient, cannot expect to be looked up to. If films were really true to life, the whole of Europe and America would deserve to be handed over as mandated territories to the Basutos, the Papuans and the Andaman pygmies. Fortunately, they are not true. We who were born in the West and live there, know it. But the untutored mind of the poor Indian does not know it. He sees the films, he thinks they represent Western reality, he cannot see why he should be ruled by criminal imbeciles. As we turned disgusted from the idiotic spectacle and threaded our way out of the crowd, that strange aquarium silence of the Javanese was broken by a languid snigger of derision. Nothing more. Just a little laugh. A word or two of mocking comment in Malay, and then once more, the silence as of fish. A few more years of Hollywood's propaganda, and perhaps we shall not get out of an Oriental crowd quite so easily.

Garoet

At this season of the year – which, the month being March, I must call spring, though it is never anything in Java but a more or less rainy midsummer – at this season the hill station of Garoet is like Paradise from dawn till lunch-time and like Scotland all the afternoon. You wake up each morning to find the sky pale blue, the row of jagged volcanoes opposite your bedroom window all rosy with sunrise, the valley in the foreground miraculously green. All morning a process of cloud-making goes on. White mountains of vapour, more fantastically shaped even than the rocks of Java, build themselves up behind the volcanoes, rise higher and ever higher into the sky, throw off white islands from their summits to float out into the welkin – until at last, after a marvellous drama of light and shadow, a slow soundless pageant of ineffable illuminations and solemn quenchings, the whole sky is overcast with vapours that, from being white and sunlit, have almost suddenly turned grey, and the whole scene below is lifeless and sad. Punctually, at about two o'clock, the first drops fall, and from that time forward the rain comes pouring down with undiminished violence till far into the night. The valley, the volcanoes, the near palms and the bamboos disappear behind grey veils of water. It is almost cold. Looking out from your veranda, you might almost believe you were sitting somewhere on the Moor of Rannoch.

But what matters Rannoch all the afternoon, if you may walk in Eden all the morning? Eden indeed; for the whole impossibly beautiful land is one great garden – but a garden on which, alas, the curse of work has fallen most heavily. Tourists in Paradise admire; but the gardeners labour incessantly. The tourists' white-skinned cousins duly see to that.

At Garoet we walked out each morning among the paradisiacal parterres. Every slope was terraced and planted with rice; and at this season all the terraces were flooded. Flights upon flights of watery steps climbed from the valleys up the hillsides. Lovingly they followed each contour of the hill, making visible and, as it were, underlining artistically the advance and recession of the curving slopes. Some of the terraces shone, within their little retaining walls of clay, like mirrors of colourless glass. In some the rice had already sprouted, and the surface of the water reflected innumerable shoots of emerald. In little torrents, from the mouth of bamboo conduits, the water poured and splashed.

But not all the fields were under water. In some they were growing sugar-cane. In some they had just cut the maize. We walked by little paths up and down through the mountainous garden. Enormous butterflies, their brown wings eyed with staring purple; butterflies metallically blue; orange and swallow-tailed; or richly funereal, as though they had been cut out of black velvet; passed and repassed with the strong swift flight of birds. In the hedges the hibiscus flowers hung open-mouthed, and their long pistils lolled like red and furry tongues. A bush covered with little flowers, star-shaped and many-coloured, blossomed along every path. But brighter than the butterflies and the flowers were the Javanese. Gaudy in their batik and fantastically patterned, they passed along the paths, they stood working in the fields. The country swarmed with them. And every two or three furlongs we would walk into a village – a hundred little houses made of bamboo and thatch and woven matting, perched on long stilts above their artificial fish ponds (for almost every house in Java has its muddy pool), and teeming with copper-coloured life. Suspended from the tops of long bamboos, the tame birds twittered in their cages. And in larger cages, raised only a few feet above the ground, we could see through the rattan bars, not birds, but – astonishingly – tall piebald sheep, one woolly prisoner in each cage.

I have never seen any country more densely populous than Java. There are places within thirty miles of London where one may walk for half an hour without meeting a soul and almost without seeing a house. But in Java one is never out of sight of man and his works. The fields are full of industrious labourers. No village seems to be more than ten minutes' walk from its nearest neighbours. Authentically paradisiacal, the landscape is very far from being a 'bowery loneliness.' By comparison with Java, Surrey seems under-populated. And for once, statistics confirm personal impressions. The best part of forty million people live on the island – the population of crowded Italy in a mountainous land of half its area.

When, in the afternoons, the rain came down and I had time to do something besides gasp with admiration at the fabulous and entirely unbelievable beauty of the landscape, I could not help thinking about this portentous populousness. I remembered those lines of Byron's – if Byron indeed it was who wrote that in every sense 'curious' poem, *Don Leon* – those classical lines, in which the whole theory of overpopulation is briefly and brutally summed up:-

> Come, MALTHUS, and in Ciceronian prose
> Show how a rutting Population grows,
> Until the produce of the Soil is spent,
> And Brats expire for lack of Aliment.

How soon the brats will start expiring in Java, I cannot say. Into what is perhaps the most fertile country in the world, they are already importing food. But that means very little. Agricultural methods may be improved; new lands opened up. In the future, who knows? Java may support eighty or a hundred, instead of a mere forty millions.

What interests me in the general problem is the particular case of the child of talent born in the lowest strata of an excessive population. What are his chances of living, in the first place; of developing and extrinsicating his talents, in the second? Brats, *tout court*, constitute the stuff of which our world is made. They may expire; but unless they do so on such an enormous scale as to imperil the whole fabric of society, it will make no difference to the world. Brats of talent, on the other hand, have it in them to change the world in one way or another. The suppression of their talent, by death or by the unpropitious circumstances of life, deprives the world of part of its vital principle of growth and change.

The lot of a human being born in the basements of any population whether excessive or small, is at the best of times unenviable. Layer upon layer of organized society lies above him; he is buried alive under a living tombstone whose interest it is to keep him buried. In the West, where the standard of living is relatively high, where the State is rich and humanitarianism is one of the principles of government, the brat of talent is given certain chances. The State provides certain educational levers and pulleys for lifting the tombstone. The child of talent – at any rate, if his talent happens to be of the examination-passing variety – can worm his way up quite early in life from the pit into which he was born.

But in the East universal primary education does not exist, the State is not run on humanitarian principles, and even if it were, would be too poor to provide the brats of talent with the costly machinery for lifting the tombstone. Nor, perhaps, are the brats even conscious of a desire to climb out of their grave. The bands of ancient custom are wound round them like a shroud; they cannot move, they do not wish to struggle. And then, consider the weight of the tombstone. In China, in India it lies like a pyramid upon them. Even if he should survive infancy – and in an Oriental city anything from three to nine hundred out of every thousand children die before completing their first year – how can the brat of talent hope, unaided, to lift the pyramid? Choirs of mute Miltons, whole regiments of guiltless Cromwells are without doubt at this moment quietly putrefying in the living graves of China and lower-caste India.

Java, like all the other Malayan countries, evolved no civilization of its own, and its barbarous record, so different from the splendid histories of China and India, does not authorize us to believe it fertile in men of talent. Still, who knows what genius may not by chance be buried under the thick layers of its population? In the pyramid above the grave of talent there are the best part of forty million stones. If I were a Javanese patriot, I should have that all too efficaciously fertilizing cannon at Batavia surreptitiously dragged from its place by the Penang Gate and thrown into the sea.

Buitenzorg

There are days in our northern winter, still days, windless, sunless and, from morning to evening twilight, uniformly illuminated under a white-grey sky, days when the whole bare country seems to glow, or to be just on the point of glowing, with an intensity of suppressed colour. It is as though a brown and earthly light were striving to break from under the clods of every ploughland; the green of the winter grass is a sulking emerald; and the leafless trees and hedges, which seem at first glance merely black, are seen by the more discerning eye as the all but opaque lanterns through which a strange, strong, quivering radiance of deepest plum colour is almost vainly shining.

In the Botanical Gardens at Buitenzorg I found myself unexpectedly reminded – in spite of the pervasive greenness, the palms, the fantastic flowers – of a winter scene in England. For the strong sullen illumination, which I have tried to describe and which is so characteristic of our December landscapes, was the same as that which lay on these tropical gardens. Under the white dead sky, the colours potentially so much stronger than any that are seen in our more rarefied landscapes, shone with a dark intensity, muffled yet violent, as though resentful of their suppression. We walked enchanted, but in a kind of horror, under huge trees heavy with foliage that seemed as though darkly and morbidly suffused with an excess of coloured life.

And when at last the sun came out, how unrestrainedly, with what a savage and immoderate exultation, the gardens responded to its greeting! The hard and shiny leaves reflected the light as though they had been made of metal, and burnished. On every tree there hung, according to the shape, the size and growth of its leaves, a multitude of shining sequins, of scythes and scimitars, of daggers and little ingots, a hundred various forms of colourless and dazzling sunshine. And where the leaves did not look towards the sun, their colour, stripped by the light of all the veils which the clouds had wrapped about it, glared out in all its intensity: the violent blue-tinged emerald of equatorial foliage.

Buitenzorg

There is a certain type of ingenious mind to which the function of decorative and applied art is simply and solely to make one object look like another and fundamentally different object. Wordsworth's Needlecase in the form of a Harp is classical. The same perverse ingenuity has begotten and is still begetting monsters as silly.

Personally, I have a weakness for these absurdities. I love the stucco that mimics marble, the washstands in the form of harpsichords, the biscuit boxes that look like Shakespeare's Complete Works tied together with an embroidered ribbon. My affection for these things prepared me to feel a special admiration for the flora of the equator. For the special and peculiar charm of tropical botany is that you can never be quite sure that it isn't zoology, or arts and crafts, or primitive religion. There are lilies in Malaya whose petals have become attenuated to writhing tentacles, so that they dangle on their stalks like perfumed spiders. There are palms whose fruits are vegetable porcupines. Dessert in Java is an affair of scarlet sea-urchins and baked potatoes: open the first – it contains the semblance of a plover's egg, hard boiled and peeled of its shell; and the potato proves to be full of a purplish custard flavoured with sherry, turpentine and chocolate. There are orchids in Singapore that might be pigeons, and others from which one recoils instinctively as though from the head of a snake. The gardens of the equator are full of shrubs that bloom with votive offerings to the Great Mother, and are fruited with coloured Easter eggs, lingams and swastikas. There are trees whose stems are fantastically buttressed to look like specimens of a late and decadent Gothic architecture; banyans pillared like the nave of a basilica; *Fici Elastiae* that trail the ropes and halters of a torture-chamber. There are red varnished leaves and leaves of shiny purple that look as though they were made of American cloth or patent leather. There are leaves cut out of pink blotting-paper; leaves whose green is piped with lines of white or rose in a manner so sketchily elegant, so daring, so characteristically 'modern,' that they are manifestly samples of the very latest furniture fabrics from Paris.

At Sea

At sea I succumb to my besetting vice of reading: to such an extent that the sand-fringed, palm-crowned islands; the immense marmoreal clouds that seem for ever poised, a sculptor's delirium, on the dividing line between chaos and accomplished form; the sunsets of Bengal lights and emeralds, of primroses and ice-cream, of blood and lamp-black; the dawns when an almost inky sea, reflecting the Eastern roses from its blue-black surface, turns the colour of wine; the stars in the soot-black sky, the nightly flashings of far-away storms beneath the horizon, the green phosphorescence on the water – all the lovely incidents of tropical seafaring float slowly past me, almost unobserved; I am absorbed in the ship's library.

Ships' libraries, I suppose, are bought either by length or by weight. Stones of prime fiction, yards of romance fill the shelves. The chief steward's key releases from their glass cages books which on land one never sees, one hardly dreams of: books about cowpunchers and sweet American heroines, all in the Great Open Air; more serious and touching novels about heroes who are misunderstood, who have appearances against them and are suspected, oh! quite unjustly, of cohabiting with pure young ladies, and who are too virtuously proud to explain, until they, the heroines and everyone else concerned have been put to the greatest possible inconvenience; sociological novels about the Modern Girl, the Poor, Night Life in London and a Decent Day's Work for a Decent Day's Wage; innumerable nondescript tales that end, instead of beginning, with slow kisses and arrangements for the wedding. Amazing works! Drifting through the tropics, I read them at the rate of three a day and found the process a liberal education.

Sometimes, surprisingly, one finds a real book, buried like a hard precious pebble in the spiritual mud of the ship's library. A real book. The discovery comes as a shock. One feels like stout Cortez, or

Robinson Crusoe confronted by the footprints, or Dr Paley when he picked up that symbolical half-hunter in the desert. What is it? How did it get there? By accident or design? In certain cases the questions admit of speciously satisfying answers. Those George Eliots, for example, so common in the Eastern seas – those can be easily accounted for by the hypothesis of a new edition, overprinted and remaindered. And perhaps the mere cheapness of the Everyman volumes would explain more than one appearance of Macaulay's *History*. Nor should one be too much astonished at finding Anatole France on the ships of the Rotterdam Lloyd; for the Dutch are polyglots and believe in culture. Miraculously so, as I discovered earlier in my wanderings. In Kashmir I met a young and charming Dutch lady who had just returned from a six months' journey of exploration in Chinese Turkestan. We were introduced, entered into conversation; she began talking, judiciously and in a flawless English, about my last novel. I was extremely gratified; but at the same time I was overwhelmed. If ever I go to Chinese Turkestan, I shall return, I am afraid, as deeply ignorant of contemporary Dutch fiction as I was before I started. But if the presence of *Thaïs* among the Dutch was explicable, the presence of Edmund Gosse's *Diversions of a Man of Letters* in the library of a small Australian vessel was almost terrifyingly unaccountable. And how on earth did the *Howard's End* of E. M. Forster introduce itself into the coastwise traffic of Burma and Malaya? How was it that Mark Rutherford became a passenger from Sandakan to Zamboanga? And why, oh why, was Bishop Berkeley travelling from Singapore with his almost eponymous namesake of *The Rosary*? After the first disquieting bewilderment, I accepted the books with thankfulness, and whenever I needed a little holiday from my studies in popular fiction, turned to them for rest and refreshment.

Among the genuine books which I discovered imbedded in a ship's library was Henry Ford's *My Life and Work*. I had never read it; I began, and was fascinated. It is easy enough in a book to apply destructive common sense to the existing fabric of social organization and then, with the aid of constructive common sense, to build up the scattered pieces into a more seemly whole. Unsystematically and in a small way I have done the thing myself. I know how easy it is. But when Ford started to apply common sense to the existing methods of industry and business he did it, not in a book, but in real life. It was only when he had smashed and rebuilt in practice that he decided to expound in a book the theory of his enormous success.

It was somewhere between the tropic and the equator that I read the book. In these seas, and to one fresh from India and Indian 'spirituality,' Indian dirt and religion, Ford seems a greater man than Buddha. In Europe, on the other hand, and still more, no doubt, in America, the way of Gautama has all the appearance of the way of Salvation. One is all for religion until one visits a really religious country. There, one is all for drains, machinery amd the minimum wage. To travel is to discover that everybody is wrong. The philosophies, the civilizations which seem, at a distance, so superior to those current at home, all prove on a close inspection to be in their own way just as hopelessly imperfect. That knowledge, which only travel can give, is worth, it seem to me, all the trouble, all the discomfort and expense of a circumnavigation.

Miri, Sarawak

It was on the point of raining when we anchored off Miri. The grey sky hung only a few feet above our masts; the sea below us was like grey oil, and between the ceiling of shifting vapours and the slowly heaving floor the air was unbreathable, like the steam of a hot bath. Half a mile away across the swell lay the land. The dark green forest came down to the water; and in little clearings, conquered from the trees, we could see a few dozens of European bungalows, a score or two of miniature Eiffel Towers marking the site of the oil wells which have called Miri into existence, a few cylindrical oil tanks, like white martello towers dotted along the coast. Out at sea, opposite a cluster of these white drums, a steamer lay at anchor; she was loading a cargo of oil from the submarine pipe-line, through which the wealth of Miri is pumped into the tankers that take it to the outer – the real – world. Beyond the near dark promontory on the right we could see, far off and sun-illuminated, a range of fantastically jagged mountains.

Grey sky, grey sea, the forest, the oil wells in the forest, the little houses among the ever-encroaching trees, and beyond them, far away through the dim hot air, the jagged mountains of Borneo – it was mournful and sinister, abysmally unreal, the landscape of a dream, of a bad dream at that. Then the rain began to fall, a few warm drops, then a shower; the mountains became the ghosts of themselves, faded, faded and were gone. The shower quickened to a downpour, and even the near coast, the oil wells and the dolls' bungalows, even the black-green forest disappeared. Walled in by falling water, we found ourselves at the centre of a little universe, whose extremest limits were not a furlong distant. It was a lively world; for in spite of the rain our steamer continued to unload its cargo into the attendant lighters. A good deal of the cargo consisted of pork – in a potential and still living form – for the consumption of the Chinese coolies working on the oil fields. Each pig was separately and closely packed in a rattan basket, significantly shaped like the sausages into which its tenant was to be so soon transformed. These wicker sausages, with their living sausage meat inside them and visible between the bars, were swung out, ten at a time, by the crane and dropped into the lighter. Three or four coolies were ready to untie the bale and arrange the separate baskets, layer by layer, in the wallowing barge. By the time it was fully loaded, there must have been six or seven successive strata of pig in the lighter. There was little squealing or struggling inside the baskets; for when unloading day arrives, the Chinese take the precaution of putting a dose of opium in the pigs' breakfast. It was only when the crane let them drop with a particularly violent bump that the drugged beasts wriggled or uttered a grunt. Mostly they lay quite still, dosing and perhaps deliciously dreaming through the entire operation of being swung through the air, let fall and dumped or rolled into place above, between, below their fellows.

The spectacle was curious and, though not precisely pleasing, certainly less deplorable than that which the man-handling of animals generally affords. The pigs might be tossed about; but plunged, like so many De Quinceys, in a trance of opium, they were not aware of it. They might be closely packed – much more closely, indeed, than they could have been packed if they had been free and struggling – but, stretched within their sausages of rattan, they were neither crushed nor suffocated. In a space where, unprisoned, no more than twenty pigs could have stood, and that to the greatest possible discomfort of each squealing victim, a hundred were now conveniently packed. By means of opium and baskets the Chinese have solved a problem in humanitarianism as well as economics.

Labuan

There had been squabblings between the deck passengers and the crew. We Olympians of the saloon were aware of it only by a dim and remote hearsay. But the fact was so true that, when we put in at Labuan, the Captain thought it necessary to pay off the two worst offenders among his Malay sailors and turn them off the ship. They took their pay, and one of them quietly departed; the other refused to move.

We saw him at a later stage of the proceedings – a young man with a face like a copper statue's, a body classically built and dressed in the height of Malay fashion. A superb specimen of humanity – but he simply wouldn't leave the ship.

The Captain sent for the dock police. Two of them, looking very smart in khaki uniform, came on board, took a good look at the young man, who sat crouched in a dark corner, sullenly ruminating his grievances, and having looked, retired. A little later four more policemen joined them, and, standing at a safe distance, the six representatives of law and order cajolingly implored the young man to come quietly. Nothing, they pointed out, was going to be done to him; he was only being asked to leave the ship; he had a right to a free passage back to Singapore. The young man said nothing, or only growled like a tiger. Discouraged, the policemen reported to the Captain that they would have to go and fetch the Resident in person: the affair was too serious for them to deal with unsupported. They trooped away. Still squatting in his corner, the young man continued to chew his bitter and maddening cud of grievance.

We, being strangers to Malaya, began to wonder, rather impatiently – for the obstinate young man was delaying our departure – why something decisive was not done about him. Nor could we understand the obvious apprehensiveness of the deck passengers and crew, the look of anxiety on the faces of the officers. In our countries men value life – their own, if not other people's. Even desperate criminals will generally come quietly when they are cornered. To shoot and, sooner or later, be shot, or hanged, would be easy. But the respect and desire for life are too strong in them; rather than violently resist, they acknowledge defeat and go off resignedly to take the unpleasant consequences of it. The Malay, on the contrary, can easily work himself up into a state of mind in which all life, including his own, seems to him valueless, when the keenest pleasure and the highest duty are to kill and be killed. Our young obstinate, crouching in his corner and ruminating his grievances, was busily preparing himself to run *amok* at the slightest provocation from his enemies. The six policemen, the deck passengers, the crew, the officers – all knew it. The officers, indeed, had reasons for knowing it particularly well. For it was only a short time before that, on a ship belonging to the same company as ours, a Malay seaman had run *amok*, for some trivially inadequate reason, and killed upwards of a dozen people, including the Captain of the vessel. The Captain, it seems, was a kindly old gentleman with a snowy beard and Christian principles. He was sent for when the trouble began, and found the Malay knife in hand, and bloody. Instead of his revolver, he used persuasion. He remonstrated, he begged the Malay to be reasonable and give up his knife. The Malay replied by sticking it into his body. The deck looked like the last act of an Elizabethan tragedy before he was finally shot down.

We had not heard this story at the time. Ignorance is bliss, and we regarded our obstinate Malay as a rather tiresome joke and wondered why every one else took him so preposterously seriously.

The Resident came at last; his forces amounted now to no less than nine policemen. It was the critical moment; the general anxiety was at its height. Would the young heathen be got off the boat without the shedding of blood? The pockets of the Captain's jacket were weighed down with fire-arms; the Resident's trousers bulged about the hip. To have produced the pistols prematurely would have been infallibly to provoke the Malay's insane fury. To pull them out too late would be no less fatal. And to fire them at all in a small and crowded ship would be a danger in itself. The situation, for those who understood it and were responsible for its developments, was disagreeably ticklish. Ignorant, we looked on in amusement. And luckily our attitude turned out to be the right and appropriate one; the drama ended as a comedy, not in blood.

When the nine policemen went below to apprehend him, the Malay slipped past them and came bounding up the companion-ladder on to the promenade deck. He probably had an idea that, if he did come to running *amok*, it would be better to kill first-class Christian passengers than third-class Moslems and devil-worshippers. But he had not yet quite succeeded in warming himself to *amok* heat. Arrived on the top deck, the forces of law and order at his heels, he glared about him, but did nothing. There was a brief colloquy with the Captain and the Resident. He stood there obstinate; he continued to shake his head. He was waiting, no doubt, for the divine afflatus that would send him ecstatically slashing and stabbing among the infidels. But the spirit of holy murder was slow to descend. The Resident saw his opportunity, nodded to his men; simultaneously the nine policemen jumped for him. The Malay made a grab for the dagger in his belt; but the spirit of murder had arrived too late. The nine had him fast. In another moment the handcuffs were round his wrists.

The strained expression dissolved from every face. Cigarettes were lighted, men began to smile, to laugh and talk. And even the handcuffed captive suddenly became good-humoured. The ferocious young savage, who had been on the verge of murder and self-destruction, was transformed, as soon as it ceased to be possible for him to run *amok*, into a merry boy. He spoke to the policemen, he laughed; and they, in the profundity of their sense of relief, laughed back at him, patted him on the shoulder, loved him. He was led off, almost a hero, down the gangway. In the midst of his escort, and followed by all the children and idlers of the town, he marched away down the road, towards the police station – the most important man, that afternoon, in Labuan.

The incident, for us, was almost enjoyable. It would have seemed a good deal less amusing if we had heard before, instead of afterwards, the story of the kindly old Captain, stabbed, with a dozen others, on his own ship, within five miles of Singapore.

The citizen of a law-abiding country, whose forty millions commit each year fewer crimes of violence than are committed in the single city of Chicago, I realized suddenly and forcibly the precarious artificiality of all that seems most solid and fundamental in our civilization, of all that we take for granted. An individual has only to refuse to play the game of existence according to the current rules to throw the rule-observing players into bewildered consternation. There is a rule against violence, against taking the law into our own hands; it is a rule which most of us observe – so many, indeed, that a great number of people go through life accepting orderliness and non-violence as part of the scheme of nature. When somebody comes into their orbit who plays the game according to 'the good old rule, the simple plan' – that is, according to no rule – they are appalled, they are at a loss what to do, they are helpless.

The War did something to alter men's attitude towards the rules, but much less than might have been expected. Men went into the fighting line not, as our generals love to say when they make speeches to public school boys, because 'Man is a Fighting Animal,' but because they were law-abiding citizens obediently doing what the State told them to do. It was the duty of the soldier to commit violence and murder upon his country's enemies; but he did these things under orders, and the doing of them hardly impaired his normal law-abidingness. Considering the fact that, for four years, half the grown men in Europe were engaged in trying to murder one another, one can only be astonished that the post-war increase in crimes of violence has not been vastly greater. That it has not is a proof of how deeply the habit of playing according to the rules has become ingrained in us. In America, the greatest part of which is removed by only a couple of generations from the mediaeval epoch of pioneering, the habit of playing according to the rules has not had time to become so deeply ingrained as in the countries whose Middle Ages of uncontrolled and lawless violence are five hundred years away. Lynching, the Ku Klux Klan, ferocious strike-breaking are American institutions, the product of American history. In England, where men abandoned the right to take the law into their own hands some two or three hundred years ago, they would be almost unthinkable. Even crime is less bloodthirsty on our side of the water; and the wholesale murderous banditry that has filled the streets of American cities with armoured cars and sharpshooters is all but unknown with us. We are fortunate in our history. How profoundly fortunate, this absurd, but potentially tragical, incident at Labuan caused me intimately to realize.

Labuan

No good pictures have ever been painted, so far as I am aware, of tropical landscapes. There are two good reasons for this, of which the first is that no good painters have ever worked in the tropics. True, the temples of Ceylon, the ghats at Benares, Penang harbour, the palms and fantastic volcanoes of Java are annually reproduced in fifty thousand water-colours. But they are the water-colours of amateurs. We have all seen them. They are the stuff that oleographs are made of. If it were not for the fact that they kept their creators harmlessly busy and contented, they ought to be put down by law. The tropics and the East are given over to amateurs. Practically every tourist who travels through them carries a paint-box. But how few serious and competent professionals ever accompany these tourists. It is difficult indeed to think of any who have ever crossed the Line. Professional painters of merit are generally poor, and their absence from the tropics may be due in part to their poverty. But poverty is not an insuperable barrier to a determined artist, and the real reason, I believe, why painters avoid the tropics is that they know them to be unpaintable. In this intrinsic unpaintableness consists the second and most adequate reason for the non-existence of decent pictures of tropical scenery.

It is a significant fact that the scenery which the enthusiastic amateur finds most picturesque, most richly 'paintable' – it is a favourite word of water-colouring spinsters – is the scenery most carefully avoided by serious professionals. Turner is one of the few great landscape-painters who ever chose to represent picturesque subjects. The rest have always preferred to meditate before more ordinary, less spectacular scenes. Italy offers extravagant beauties; but the English have obstinately gone on painting in the placid home counties of their own islands; the French have never wandered further than to the bare hills of Provence; the Flemings have found their subjects within a hundred miles of Antwerp; the Dutch have stuck to their polders and estuaries. Strange at first sight, the phenomenon is easily explained. A picturesque landscape (which is, by definition, a landscape naturally possessing some of the qualities of a man-made picture) is one which inevitably imposes itself on the painter. In the face of its overwhelming grandiosities, its naturally dramatic character, its ready-made composition, he finds himself being reduced to the rôle of a merely passive recording instrument. That is all very well for the amateurs. A picturesque landscape excuses them from making any creative gesture of their own; all they have to do is to sit down and faithfully copy. But the serious painter does not want to be imposed upon by his subject; he wants to impose himself on it. He does not want to be excused from making an effort of his own. On the contrary, he feels impelled by his talent to make the creative gesture which moulds the chaos of the world into an ordered and human cosmos – which turns nature into art. That is why he avoids the rich, the picturesque, the imposing, the dramatic. He wants a plain, and almost neutral subject, on which he can impress his own human ideas of composition and harmony, his own conception of the grand and the dramatic. The quiet English downland is less definitely formed than the prodigious landscapes of the Alban Hills; Flanders and the Lower Seine are more malleable, so to speak, more amenable to artistic treatment, than the Bay of Naples; Delft is more easily digested by the intellect than Tivoli. Turner, it is true, could swallow Italy and turn it into art; but then he was a kind of spiritual ostrich. Most painters prefer a lighter diet.

What is true of Italian is true, *a fortiori*, of tropical landscape. The picturesqueness of the most 'paintable' parts of the tropical Orient is so excessive, that the serious artist must feel, when confronted with them, as though he were being bullied, robbed of his initiative, dictated to. He might enjoy looking at Java or Borneo; but he would never dream of painting there. If he wanted subjects to paint he would go back to Essex or Normandy.

Tropical landscapes, besides being too picturesque to be turned into good pictures, are also too rich. Things in this part of the world have a way of being unmanageably thick on the ground. There is no room in a painting for the profusion that exists in tropical reality. The painter of the average tropical scene would have to begin by leaving nine-tenths of reality out of his picture. That was what

Gauguin, one of the few good painters who ever practised in the tropics, habitually did. If he had not, there would have been no seeing the wood for the inordinate quantity of the trees.

The various aspects of the tropical world still await their interpreters. A hundred admirable painters have taught us to know what European landscapes really look like. But the artistic essence of the tropical Orient remains to be distilled. Java awaits its Gainsborough and its Constable; Benares its Canaletto. Sportsmen are plentiful in the Malayan forests, and sometimes they carry sketch-books as well as rifles. But the Corot who will tell us how those forests should be seen has not yet walked among their green and leech-infested shadows. We are compelled to see the tropics either in terms of the snapshot, the amateur's imitation of the oleograph, or of the steamship company's poster. Palm-trees, Reckitt's blue sky and ocean, purple mountains, silver or golden sands – as far as it goes, the steamship poster (which is at least the work of a professional) is remarkably truthful. When I saw the immense *Laconia* steaming into the harbour of Labuan, I could have believed myself in a London tube station, looking at the advertisements of winter cruises in the South Seas. But there is something more subtly and essentially real to be got out of the tropics than the amateur's water-colour and the steamship poster – something which we can all dimly recognize, but to which no professional seer has yet taught us to give a definite outline. English landscapes were beautiful before Gainsborough who made the loveliness clearly visible, who gave it a name and a definition.

The pest pictures of the tropics are in books. There is more of the essence and the inward reality of the tropics in a book by Conrad or Herman Melville, more in a good passage by H. M. Tomlinson, more even in the rather maudlin Pierre Loti than in any existing painting of the places they describe. But description, even the description of the most accomplished writers, is very unsatisfying and inadequate. And it is no use practising symbolical evocations on those who have never seen the realities which it is desired to evoke. For those who have eaten a mutton pie, it is all very well to speak of 'dreams of fleecy flocks, pent in a wheaten cell.' But we may be quite sure that the congenital vegetarian would never succeed, with the help of only this recipe, in preparing the homely dish. The art of evocation is an admirable one; but when there is nothing in the reader's mind to be evoked, it is practised in vain. It is no use whistling to a dog which isn't there. Symbolical evocation will never create a true picture of the tropics in the minds of those who have passed their lives in Bayswater. No, the only way of explaining to those who have never been there – as well as to those who have – what the tropics are really like, would be to distil them into pictures. The thing has never been done, and it seems to me quite probable, for the reasons I have already given, that it never will be.

Kudat, North Borneo

The steamers from Singapore call at all the principal ports of British North Borneo. But the tourist who supposes that he will be able, at those places, to study those romantic beings 'the Wild Men of Borneo,' is profoundly mistaken. At Kudat, it is true, we actually did see two small and dirty people from the interior, hurrying apprehensively along the relatively metropolitan street of that moribund little port as though in haste to be back in their forests. Poor specimens they were; but we had to be content with them. They were the nearest approach to wild men we had seen or were destined to see, the only genuine and aboriginal Borneans. For the rest, we saw only Chinese. Except for a few Englishmen they are the sole inhabitants of the ports. Labuan and Jesselton, Kudat and Sandakan are merely Chinese colonies. And behind the ports, in the land that has been conquered from the forest – there too they are to be found. With the Javanese they work the big company-owned plantations, they cultivate small holdings of their own. And every-where the shopkeepers, the merchants are Chinese. It is the same all over the archipelago and in the Malay peninsula. Not European capital so much as Chinese labour and perseverance is developing the East Indies. Abolish the Chinese, and European colonization would be impossible. Or at least it would be a merely platonic and honorary colonization. Flags might be planted without the assis-tance of the Chinese – but not rubber. It is pleasant, no doubt, it is soul-satisfying to look at the coloured bunting flapping in the tropical breeze. But it is still pleasanter to draw dividends. For this keener pleasure Europeans must thank the Chinamen.

Sandakan

Sandakan, like Jesselton, Kudat and, I suppose, all the other sea-coast towns of North Borneo, is a Chinese colony governed by a few white men inhabiting the bungalows in the suburbs. It is a picturesque place, has a marvellous natural harbour with a great red rock, like a second Gibraltar, to guard its entrance, and is the port and capital of a little hinterland of coconut groves, rubber and tobacco plantations. A club-house and a golf course proclaim it to be, if not a part of the British Empire, at least a protectorate. (Examined in detail and at close quarters, our far-flung Empire is seen to consist of several scores of thousands of clubs and golf courses, dotted at intervals, more or less wide, over two-fifths of the surface of the planet. Large blond men sit in the clubs, or swipe the white ball down clearings in the jungle; blackamoors of various shades bring the whiskey and carry round the niblicks. The map is painted red. And to the casual observer, on the spot, that is the British Empire.) But to return to Sandakan. Besides a club and a golf course, it possesses four steam-rollers and a superbly metalled road, eleven miles long. At the eleventh milestone, the road collides with what seems an impenetrable wall of forest and comes abruptly to an end. You get out of your car and, examining the wall of verdure, find it flawed by a narrow crevice; it is a path. You edge your way in and are at once swallowed up by the forest. The inside of Jonah's whale could scarcely have been hotter, darker or damper. True, the jungle monster sometimes opens its mouth to yawn; there is a space between the trees, you have a glimpse of the sky, a shaft of thick yellow sunlight comes down into the depths. But the yawns are only brief and occasional. For the greater part of our stroll in the belly of the vegetable monster, we walked in a hot twilight. It was silent too. Very occasionally a bird would utter a few notes – or it might have been a devil of the woods, meditatively whistling to himself, as he prepared some fiendishly subtle and ingenious booby trap to terrify the human trespassers on his domain.

Nature is all very well half-way to the pole. Kept on short rations, she behaves decorously. But feed her up, give her huge doses of the tonic tropical sunlight, make her drunk with tropical rain, and she gets above herself. If Wordsworth had been compelled to spend a few years in Borneo, would he have loved nature as much as he loved her on the banks of Rydal Water? If the *Excursion* had been through equatorial Africa, instead of through Westmorland, old William's mild pantheism would have been, I suspect, a little modified.

It was with a feeling of the profoundest relief that I emerged again from the green gullet of the jungle and climbed into the waiting car. The Chinese chauffeur started the machine and we drove away, very slowly (for in Sandakan you hire a car by the hour, not by the mile; the drivers are marvellously cautious), we drove positively majestically down the eleven-mile road. I thanked God for steam-rollers and Henry Ford.

The Southern Philippines

The Dutch and English were never such ardent Christians that they thought it necessary to convert, wholesale and by force, the inhabitants of the countries which they colonized. The Spaniards, on the contrary, did really believe in their extraordinary brand of Catholic Christianity; they were always crusaders as well as freebooters, missionaries as well as colonists. Wherever they went, they have left behind them their religion, and with it (for one cannot teach a religion without teaching many other things as well) their language and some of their habits.

The Philippines were Spanish for upwards of three hundred years. They were neglected, it is true, they were governed at one remove, through Mexico; still they were Spanish. That is a fact of which you become aware the moment you set foot on the island of Sulu, the southernmost and, as it happens, the least Hispaniolized and Christian of the Philippines. At Zamboanga you are made more certain of it. At Manila it is fairly drummed into you. The landscape is familiarly tropical and East Indian. (Sulu is like a miniature Java,

impossibly beautiful.) But the world into which you have stepped –
you realize it at once – is unlike anything of which you have yet had
experience in the equatorial Orient. It is Spain – diluted, indeed,
distorted, based on Malayan savagery and overlaid with American-
ism, but still indubitably Spain. The Dutch have been in Java for
more than three centuries. Their colonists have freely intermarried
with the natives; many have made the island their permanent home,
have lived and died there and left their families behind them. But
Java remains Javanese. The people have retained their clothes, their
language, their religion; even in the towns, at the cosmopolitan
ports, they are totally un-Dutch, just as the Malays of the peninsula,
the Dyaks and Dusuns of Sarawak and North Borneo are totally
un-English. If we had been as passionately Anglican as the Spaniards were passionately Catholic, the urban Malays would now be
wearing cotton plus-fours, talking cockney and, on Sundays, singing
hymns A. and M. But – luckily or unluckily, I do not know – we
were only tepidly Anglican. The Malay continues to wear his skirt,
to talk Malayan, to worship Mohammed's new-fangled Allah and
the immemorial ghosts and devils of his native forest.

Landing at Jolo (one pronounces it Holo), the capital of Sulu
island, we found ourselves in a small decaying Spanish town. There
were public gardens with fountains and a group of comically
sublime and allegorical modern statuary. A noise of nasal singing
issued from a church; we looked in and saw a choir of small brown
urchins being taught by a brown choirmaster to chant the canticles
and responses. Filippino ladies, dressed like the beauties whose
portraits one sees on the inside of cigar-box lids, swam past. Their
long trailing skirts were looped up on one side to show the under
petticoat. Their bodices of stiff muslin were amazing relics of the
eighteenth century, sweepingly cut to reveal a brown décolleté and
fitted with enormous puffed sleeves, like the wings of butterflies or
the fins of some more than usually improbable kind of tropical fish.
While the girls and the younger women wore their hair 'up,' their
elders, preposterously, kept it hanging in a long black cataract down
their backs. As for the men, those who were not Filippinos and
wearing the most elegant of white duck suits, were dressed – it
depended upon their tribal and national affinities – either in skin-
tight fleshings, a gaudily coloured sash or belt, a little toreador

jacket and a coloured bandana for the head, or else – flying to the other sartorial extreme – in more than Oxford, more even than Mexican trousers of brightly coloured silk (pale pink, green, yellow, orange), a larger sash, generally ornamented with an enormous kris, a still more handsome bull-fighter's jacket and, over the bandana, a colossal hat.

Fantastic garments! But surely not of indigenous devising. Nowhere but in the Philippines do the Malays dress themselves as toreadors and cowboys. The least original of people, they have borrowed their clothes from their conquerors and enemies. The fancy dress of the Sulus and the fierce proud Moros, who were the Spaniards' most dangerous foes, has been taken from a Spanish-Mexican wardrobe. And that extraordinary swagger, those noble attitudes – those too are Spanish. And then the language. The country folk, of course, have never learnt it. But it rumbles nobly in the urban streets and shops. Nor, as we discovered, is it the Filippinos alone who speak it. We had made our way along the rickety wooden pier on which, perched above the sea, the Chinese traders have their shops and dwelling-houses, and were seeking to buy some of those enormous pearl shells for which the island of Sulu is celebrated. We found them after much searching in the back rooms of a Chinese shop – mountainous heaps of the shining nacreous shells. We sifted the treasure and selected as many as we wanted. Then came the time to pay. We turned to the Chinaman. He knew no English. Our two words of Malay were spoken in vain. In despair we tried Spanish. He responded. English and yellow Celestial, we conducted our little haggle in pidgin Castilian.

Manila

Manila is the capital of an American colony. That is a fact of which I was not for long permitted to remain in doubt. Within three hours of my landing, I had been interviewed by nine reporters, representing the entire press, English and Spanish, of the city. I was asked what I thought of Manila, of the Filippino race, of the political problems of the islands – to which I could only reply by asking my interviewers what *they* thought about these subjects and assuring them, when they had told me, that I thought the same. My opinions were considered by all parties to be extraordinarily sound.

When this sort of thing happens – and fortunately it very seldom happens except on United States territory – I am always set thinking of that curious scale of values by which, in this preposterous world, men and things are appraised. Take, for example, the case of the literary man. (I am a literary man myself, and so the matter interests me.) The literary man is invested, it seems to me, with a quite disproportionate aura of importance and significance. Literary men fairly pullulate in *Who's Who*. They are more numerously represented in that remarkable book than any other class of notorieties, with the possible exception of peers and baronets. Almost nobody who has sold five thousand copies and had a good review in the *Times Literary Supplement*, is missing from its pages. A dispassionate observer from Mars would be led, by a study of *Who's Who*, to suppose that a certain gift of the gab was the most important quality an inhabitant of this planet could possess. But is it?

Art and the artist have become tremendously important in our modern world. Art is spoken of with respect, almost with reverence as though it were something sacred; and every adolescent aspires to be an artist, as regularly and inevitably as every child aspires to be an engine-driver. Art is one of the things that have flowed in to fill the vacuum created in the popular mind by the decay of established religion. The priest, whose confessional functions have passed to the lawyer and the doctor, has bequeathed his mystical prestige, his dignity as a guardian of the sacraments, to the artist. Hence the enormous number of literary names in *Who's Who*. Hence the inter-viewers who flock to ask the wandering novelist his opinion about things of which he must necessarily be incompetent to speak. The obscure scientist, whose mental equipment may be incomparably superior to that of the literary man, is left in peace. The public, being incapable of understanding what he is talking about, takes no interest in him. He must achieve something spectacular before hostesses ask him out and reporters come to meet him at the station. The practical man is hardly more esteemed (unless, of course, he happens to be immensely rich) than the man of science. To many people a man who writes poetry (even very bad poetry) and has an opinion about post-impressionism, is necessarily more intelligent than even a first-class engineer, or capable official, or the organizer of a great industry. Doctors and mill-owners, government servants and lawyers can cross the seas without running the slightest risk of being buttonholed at every port by a crowd of newspaper men. They may be more intelligent than the man of letters, they may be better men doing work infinitely more valuable than his. They may be qualified by special knowledge to speak with authority about the things which reporters love to discuss; but they will be permitted to land unmolested. Their work lacks the prestige which attaches to art; moreover it is private work, confined to one place and to the actual time of its achievement. The novelist's work is public; it exists simultaneously in many thousands of places: it can be looked at over a long space of time – as long indeed (if his vogue lasts) as wood pulp can hold together.

As a mere spectator of the world, not an actor in it – one who looks on and forms opinions of what other people are doing, but does nothing himself – I feel the profoundest admiration for those who act, who impress their will on stubborn things, not merely on yielding ideas, who wield power over men directly, and not impersonally as the writer does by wielding power over weak words. I admire and envy; but I do not aspire to be their rivals. Born a spectator, I should make the poorest performer. I have a certain talent for using the opera-glasses and making appropriate comments. I have none for acting. It is better to be content with doing what one can do, than to make a fool of oneself by trying to do what one can't. If I were set down to do some of the serious practical work that has to be done in order that spectators can watch the comedy in safety and comfort, I should behave like that Burmese king of whom it is written in the *Glass Palace Chronicle*: 'For the sake of his concubines he composed the Paramatthabinda, that they might know of mind and the qualities of mind, matter, *nirvana*, forms of being and personality. He would not even lend an ear to the affairs of the villages or kingdom. Whenever there was an inquiry to be made, power exercised, or point of law determined, he caused his son, Uzana, the heir apparent, to dispose thereof.'

I admire Uzana; but oh! I understand, I sympathize with, I have a fellow-feeling for his poor father. How infinitely pleasanter, if one happens to be born with a speculative mind and a gift of the gab, to chat with one's concubines about *nirvana* and the qualities of mind than to bother oneself with the affairs of the villages! Uzana was undoubtedly the better man; but his father, the distinguished author of 'Metaphysics in the Harem' and 'Kant for Concubines,' must have been the one whom everybody wanted to meet, who received letters from distant female correspondents, who got asked out to dinner, interviewed on the wharf and snapshotted walking with a friend in the Park. All these things would happen to him; and he – for I take it that he had really and seriously thought about the qualities of mind and the forms of matter – he would be astonished every time and, thinking of Uzana, he would feel embarrassed and even rather ashamed, as though he were an impostor.

PART THREE
The Pacific

Shanghai

I have seen places that were, no doubt, as busy and as thickly populous as the Chinese city in Shanghai, but none that so overwhelmingly impressed me with its business and populousness. In no city, West or East, have I ever had such an impression of dense, rank, richly clotted life. Old Shanghai is Bergson's *élan vital* in the raw, so to speak, and with the lid off. It is Life itself. Nothing more intensely living can be imagined. There are as many people – there are very likely more – in an equal area of London or Lahore, of Glasgow or Bombay; but there is not so much life. Each individual Chinaman has more vitality, you feel, than each individual Indian or European, and the social organism composed of these individuals is therefore more intensely alive than the social organism in India or the West. Or perhaps it is the vitality of the social organism – a vitality accumulated and economized through centuries by ancient habit and tradition – perhaps it is the intense aliveness and strength of the Chinese civilization, which give to individual Chinamen their air of possessing a superabundance of life beyond the vital wealth of every other race. So much life, so carefully canalized, so rapidly and strongly flowing – the spectacle of it inspires something like terror. All this was going on when we were cannibalistic savages. It will still be going on – a little modified, perhaps, by Western science, but not much – long after we in Europe have simply died of fatigue. A thousand years from now the seal-cutters will still be engraving their seals, the ivory workers still sawing and polishing; the tailors will be singing the merits of their cut and cloth, even as they do to-day; the spectacled astrologers will still be conjuring silver out of the pockets of bumpkins and amorous courtesans; there will be a bird market, and eating-houses perfumed with delicious cooking, and chemists' shops with bottles full of dried lizards, tigers' whiskers, rhinoceros horns and pickled salamanders; there will be patient jewellers and embroiderers of faultless taste, shops full of marvellous crockery, and furriers who can make elaborate patterns and pictures out of variously coloured fox-skins; there will still be letter-writers at the street corners and men whose business it is to sit in their open shops inscribing words of ancient wisdom on long red scrolls – and the great black ideographs will still be as perfectly written as they are to-day, or were a thousand years ago, will be thrown on to the red paper with the same apparent recklessness, the same real and assured skill, by a long fine hand as deeply learned in the hieratic gestures of its art as the hand of the man who is writing now. Yes, it will all be there, just as intensely and tenaciously alive as ever – all there a thousand years hence, five thousand, ten. You have only to stroll through old Shanghai to be certain of it. London and Paris offer no such certainty. And even India seems by comparison provisional and precarious.

Japan

It was grey when we landed at Kobe, and the air was cold and smelt of soot. There was deep mud in the streets. A little while after we had stepped on shore, it began to rain. We might have been landing at Leith in the height of a Scotch November.

Lifted above the mud on stilt-like clogs, little men paddled about the streets; they were dressed in Inverness capes of grey or brown silk and cheap felt hats. Women in dressing-gowns, with high-piled, elaborately architectured hair, like the coiffure of an old-fashioned barmaid, dyed black, toddled beside them, leading or carrying on their backs gaudily dressed children whose round expressionless button-faces were like the faces of little Eskimoes. It seemed, certainly, an odd sort of population to be inhabiting Leith. Reluctantly we had to admit that we were indeed in the Extreme Orient, and the flowers in the shops had to be accepted as a sufficient proof that this funereal wintry day was really a day in the month of Cherry Blossom.

We got into the train and for two hours rolled through a grey country, bounded by dim hills and bristling with factory chimneys. Every few miles the sparse chimneys would thicken to a grove, with, round their feet – like toadstools about the roots of trees – a sprawling collection of wooden shanties: a Japanese town. The largest of these fungus beds was Osaka.

It was late in the afternoon when we arrived at Kyoto, the ancient capital, 'the Art City of Japan' (we had been well primed before starting with touristic literature). Declining the proffered taxi, we climbed into rickshaws, the better to observe the town. It was only feebly drizzling. Dressed like Anglo-Saxon messengers in blue jerkins and tights, our coolies drew us splashing through the mud. Kyoto is like one of those mining camps one sees on the movies, but two or three hundred times as large as any possible Wild Western original. Little wooden shack succeeds little wooden shack interminably, mile after mile; and the recession of the straight untidy roads is emphasized by the long lines of posts, the sagging electric wires that flank each street, like the trees of an avenue. All the cowboys in the world could live in Kyoto, all the Forty-Niners. Street leads into identical street, district merges indistinguishably into district. In this dreary ocean of log-cabins almost the only White Houses are the hotels.

For a few hours that evening it ceased to rain. We took the opportunity to explore the city on foot. The streets were well lighted, the shops – and almost every one of the hundred thousand shacks in Kyoto is a shop – were mostly open. We walked through the city, seeing the commercial life steadily and seeing it almost whole. It was like walking, ankle-deep in mud, through an enormous Woolworth's bazaar. Such a collection of the cheap and shoddy, of the quasi-genuine and the imitation-solid, of the vulgar and the tawdry, I have never seen. And the strange thing was that, in Kyoto, even the real, the sound, the thoroughly *pukka* had an air of flimsiness and falsity. Looking at the most expensive kimonos with a lifetime of wear woven into their thick silk, you would swear that they were things of wood-pulp. The ivories resemble celluloid; the hand embroideries have the appearance of the machine-made article. The genuine antiques – the ones you see in the museums, for there are none elsewhere – look as though they had been fabricated yesterday. This is due partly to the fact that in recent years we have become so familiar with the conventional forms of Japanese art turned out on machines by the million for the penny bazaar market, that we cannot associate them with anything but cheapness and falsity; partly too, I think, to a certain intrinsic feebleness and vulgarity in the forms themselves. That sobriety, that strength, that faultless refinement which are the characteristics of Chinese art, and which give to the cheapest piece of Chinese earthenware, the most ordinary embroidery or carving or lettering, a magistral air of artistic importance and significance, are totally lacking, so it seems to me, in the art of Japan. The designs of Japanese fabrics are garish and pretentious; the sculpture even of the best periods is baroque; the pottery which in China is so irreproachable both in hue and shape is always in Japan just not 'right.' It is as though there were some inherent vice in Japanese art which made the genuine seem false and the expensive shoddy.

Factories, smoke, innumerable Woolworths, mud – were these Japan? We were assured they were not. The 'real' Japan (all countries have a 'real' self, which no stranger can ever hope to see) was something different, was somewhere else. Looking at the celebrated Cherry Dances in Kyoto, we were almost ready to believe it. The costumes, it is true, were extraordinarily vulgar and garish. The scenery in Western style – the Western style of the pre-War provincial pantomime – was deplorable. Any self-respecting producer of revues in London or New York could have staged a far more adequate Old Japan. But he could not have got the dancing. That was an enchantment. A chorus of thirty or forty geishas, drilled to a pitch of almost Prussian efficiency, their farded faces impassive as white masks, performed a ballet that was the formalization of the gestures of courtesy, that was polite conversation made more gracefully polite, that was the apotheosis of good manners at the tea-table. And hardly less lovely were the movements of the orchestra. In Europe one pays to listen to music; in Japan one pays to see it played. When European performers make their appearance upon the platform, one generally wants to shut one's eyes; in a Japanese concert-room, on the other hand, one desires to keep one's eyes wide open and to close one's ears. Not that the music is unpleasant. What I heard at Kyoto might have been the remote and geological ancestor of Russian music. It stood in relation to Rimsky-Korsakov as pithecanthropus stands to man; it was a kind of *ur*-Stravinsky, a fossil and primitive form of the genus Mussorgsky. Not unpleasing, I repeat, but after a while a little boring. The guitars, on which twenty geishas played with plectrums that looked like ivory combs, were singularly poor in tone. And the tambourines, the cymbals and the drums, which were being played by twenty of their sisters on the opposite side of the hall, beat out only the simplest and most obvious rhythms. No, the orchestra was not much to listen to. But what a ravishment to behold! They were as well drilled as the ballerinas. The twenty guitar players sat in identically the same position, and when they combed the strings of their instruments their hands performed the same movements simultaneously, as though they were the synchronously moving parts of one machine. Similar machines actuated the eight hour-glass-shaped tambourines, the eight small kettle-drums, the two sets of cymbals, the two little gongs. Most exquisite of all were the drummers. They knelt in front of their instruments as though before a row of little gods. Each held a pair of enormous white drumsticks, so thick that the tiny hands could hardly grasp them. With these, in unison, they tapped the little gods before whom they knelt; and the little drum gods answered them, boom boom – a response, it must be admitted, rather more clear and comprehensible than that which deities are accustomed to vouchsafe to their worshippers. But then the ritual of these Japanese adorers was so beautiful that it could hardly fail to be magically compelling. Their arms, prolonged by the enormous white drumsticks, were held out before them almost at full stretch. And when they beat, they beat from the shoulder, lifting and letting fall the whole arm. But 'letting fall' is not the right expression; it connotes a loose and undeliberate movement, and the drummers did nothing undeliberately. On the contrary, each stroke was applied with a perfectly controlled precision. Tap, tap, tap-a-tap, tap; they touched the drum face as though they were fitting into position, one by one, the tesserae, now large, now small, of an elaborate mosaic.

Perhaps these dancers, these exquisitely disciplined musicians, were the 'real' Japan. Perhaps, too, it existed in the country which we saw on our way to Yokohama. The sun had come out at last. The sky was palely blue and alive with clouds that trailed great indigo shadows across the earth beneath them. It was an almost Italian country of abrupt hills and lakes and mountain-encircled plains. A paler variety of our mustard was blooming in the fields. Great expanses of primrose yellow covered the plains to the edge of the blue lakes, to the feet of the dim blue mountains. The mustard seemed to me far more impressively beautiful than the cherry blossom. The near hills were brown, steep, almost bare, their crests fringed with a growth, not of the Tuscan unbrella pine, but of the trees which figure so largely in the native woodcuts, the ragged, yet strangely elegant, pine-trees, whose silhouette against the sky is like a Chinese ideograph. To one familiar with the Celestial symbols, the whole landscape, I liked to fancy, would be an open book. Wisdom and poetry would sprout for him on every hill. Or perhaps, who knows? the trees might just be saying, 'Foreign Devil, Foreign Devil,' and repeating it monotonously, mile after mile. The second, I am afraid, is the more probable hypothesis. We rolled on, through miles of innumerable little rice fields laboriously embanked to hold the water with which they were being flooded; among sloping plantations of tea shrubs, round and shinily green, like bushes of clipped box; through luminous plains of mustard and young green corn; past villages of thatched houses beautifully set among the trees. And every twenty miles or so, we would catch glimpses of a thing which seemed, at first, only a white cloud among the clouds of the horizon, a pale small ghost, but a ghost which, at every glimpse, became more definite, clearer, larger, until – hours after we had had our earliest sight of it – it stood shining high above us, a huge white cone, girdled with clouds, a miracle of regular and geometrical form among the chaotic hills which it overtopped, the sacred mountain of Japan, Fujiyama. We saw it first at noon, a tiny cloud melting into the clouds; and at sunset we were looking back on it, an enormous mass rising clear of all vapours, naked and perfect, into the coloured sky. Was this the 'real' Japan? I suppose so.

But a little later, at Yokohama, we were plunged again, head over ears, into the unreal. If Kyoto looks like a mining camp, Yokohama after the earthquake looks like a mining camp that has not yet been finished. There are dust-heaps among the shanties, there are holes in the roadways, there are unbuilt bridges. But in a little while, when the mass is all cleared up and the damage repaired, it will be just like Kyoto – miles of dreary ill-kept roads, hundreds of thousands of ugly little wooden shanties, and every shanty a shop and every shop a Woolworth. But there are differences of quality, there is a higher and a lower, even among Woolworths. At Kyoto the shops had looked like threepenny bazaars. At Yokohama they were only penny ones.

We boarded our ship with thankfulness. 'Real' Japan had been delightful. But there had been more of the unreal than of the real, and the unreal, moreover, was obviously so much the more significant and important that it had quite eclipsed the real. In every country the places, the people, the institutions which are said by lovers of that country to constitute its 'real' self are the least characteristic and significant. Cornwall and county families and the Anglican Church may be the esoterically 'real' England. But the England that matters, that makes history, that impresses itself on the world and casts its shadow into the future, is represented by Lancashire, Trade Unions and Big Business Men. It is the same, I suppose, with Japan. Fuji and village life, traditional dances and cultured gentlemen of leisure, are what the lovers of Japan would have us believe to be the 'real' thing. But it is the unreal Japan, the wholesale producer of shoddy, which is at present projecting itself on history. Not the dancers, not the cultured and religious gentlemen, but the manufacturers of shoddy direct the country's policy. And in the enormous mining-camp cities more and more of the Japanese are being transformed, for good or for evil, from peasants and craftsmen into proletarian factory hands, the brothers of all the other proletarian workers of the world. The future of Japan, as of every other country, depends on its 'unreal' self. Some day, in the Utopian future, when things are very different from what they are now, English and Japanese patriots, desirous of exalting their respective countries, will point, not to Cornwall or Fuji, not to the county families or the descendants of the Tea Masters, but to Manchester and Osaka, to the cotton spinners and the weavers of silk. 'Here,' they will say, 'here is the real England, the real Japan.' Progress may be defined in this connection as the gradual transformation of what we now call 'unreal' into something sufficiently noble and decent to be styled 'real.' Meanwhile we have the misfortune to live in a world in which all that is historically significant is so repulsive that we are compelled, if we have any pride in our country or our human species, to practise a wholesale Christian Science on it and deny it reality.

Japan

Accustomed to deploring and at the same time taking advantage of the low standards of living current elsewhere in the East, the traveller who enters Japan is rudely surprised when he finds himself asked to pay his rickshaw coolie a wage which would not be despised in Europe. To travel otherwise than by tram through the streets of a Japanese city is a luxury. I was glad, for the sake of the rickshaw coolies, that it should be so; for my own, I must confess, I was sorry. To the slave-owners, slavery seems a most delightful institution.

On the Pacific

Each evening before dinner as we zig-zag down the long corridor towards our cabin, now labouring uphill as the liner dips to port in the slow swell, now racing downwards as it rights itself and dips again to starboard, we hear behind our neighbours' closed doors a curious dry clicking sound. It is a sound which, in a convent, one would attribute to the rapid and multitudinous telling of beads. But a liner is not a convent, and trans-Pacific passengers are no more pious than ordinary folk. Those clickings are not the record of muttered *Paternosters* and high-speed *Aves*. They are the sound of ice being rattled in cocktail shakers. We are on an American ship, and when we want to drink we must do so in our cabins and from our own private cellars. And how ardently one does want to drink when one is not allowed to. A childish desire to do what is prohibited is stronger than taste and habit. I, who abhor whiskey, have a large bottle of it in my trunk. And every evening we gravely sit down in our cabin to drink some of the champagne with which certain kind American friends, with a thoughtful foresight born of their knowledge of Prohibition, presented us before we left Japan.

At Sea

Familiarity blunts astonishment. Fishes do not marvel at water; they are too busy swimming in it. It is the same with us. We take our Western civilization for granted and find nothing intrinsically odd or incongruous in it. Before we can realize the strangeness of our surroundings, we must deliberately stop and think.

But moments come when that strangeness is fairly forced upon our notice, moments when an anomaly, a contradiction, an immense incongruity is suddenly illumined by a light so glaring that we cannot fail to see it. Such a moment came to me as I was crossing the Pacific. It was the first morning out of Yokohama. Coming out of my cabin, I was handed the day's bulletin of wireless news. I unfolded the typewritten sheet and read: 'Mrs X, of Los Angeles, girl wife of Dr X, aged 79, has been arrested for driving her automobile along the railroad track, whistling like a locomotive.' This piece of information had been transmitted through the ethereal holes between the molecules of air. From a broadcasting station more than five thousand miles away it had come to our ship in rather less time than it would have taken the sound of my voice to travel from one end of the promenade deck to the other. The labours of half a dozen men of genius, of hundreds of patient and talented investigators, had gone to creating and perfecting the means for achieving this miracle. To what end? That the exploits of young Mrs X, of Los Angeles, might be instantaneously known to every traveller on all the oceans of the globe. The ether reverberated with the name of Mrs X. The wave that bore it broke against the moon and the planets, and rippled on towards the stars and the ultimate void. Faraday and Clerk Maxwell had not lived in vain.

The wise men of antiquity (so say the Indians) knew all that we have learned about nature, and a great deal more besides. But they kept their science to themselves, or revealed it only in enigmas which cannot be interpreted except in the light of a previous knowledge of the answers. They were afraid that – men being what they are – their discoveries might be put to bad or futile uses. The ordinary man, they argued, is not to be trusted with the power which comes of knowledge. They withheld their science.

Being prejudiced in favour of the West and of the present, I have no great belief in the scientific attainments of the ancient sages of the Orient. But their wisdom is undeniable. The fruits of knowledge are abused and wasted; it is, alas, only too obvious. Disinterested men have given their lives to the search for truth, and we have turned their discoveries to the service of murder, or employed them to create a silly entertainment. The modern civilization of the West, which is the creation of perhaps a hundred men of genius, assisted by a few thousand intelligent and industrious disciples, exists for the millions, whose minds are indistinguishable in quality from those of the average humans of the palaeolithic age. The ideas of a handful of super-men are exploited so as to serve the profit and pleasure of the innumerable subter-men, or men *tout court*. The contemporary cave man listens in on instruments which he owes to the inspired labours of superior and, by comparison, divine intelligences. Negroid music shoots across the void into his ears, and the wisdom of such sages as Dr Frank Crane; racing results and bed-time stories and the true tale of a young Mrs X, of Los Angeles. The fire of Prometheus is put to the strangest uses. Gods propose, men dispose. The world in which we live may not be the best of all possible worlds: it is certainly the most fantastic.

Not being a super-man myself, I took the liveliest interest in young Mrs X. After being arrested for whistling like a locomotive – whether by means of an instrument or with the unaided vocal cords was never made clear – she was bailed out of prison by her husband, the aged doctor. The time came for the hearing of her case. Mrs X told the doctor that she proposed to forfeit her (or rather his) recognizances and run away. The doctor protested. Mrs X then began to smash the furniture. The aged doctor telephoned for the police; they came, and Mrs X was rearrested on charges of assault. We on the Pacific waited in a dreadful suspense. A few days later, as we were crossing the hundred and eightieth meridian, we learned to our profound relief that a reconciliation had taken place. Aged Dr X had withdrawn his charge; the girl wife had gone home quietly. What happened about the whistling business we never learned. The anonymous powers which purvey wireless news are strangely capricious. The name of Mrs X no longer rippled out towards Aldebaran and the spiral nebulae. In the next morning's bulletin there was a little paragraph announcing the declaration of the General Strike. And Bébé Daniels had fallen off her horse and received contusions.

PART FOUR
America

San Francisco

Reporters were lying in wait on the quay to ask me what I thought about the General Strike. I told them that I had been at sea for the last month and was therefore entirely ignorant of current English affairs. That made no difference, they assured me; they wanted my opinion all the same. I gave them my prejudices, which are Fabian and mildly labourite. They thanked me, took some photographs and departed. The photographs appeared in the evening papers. They bore a certain resemblance to the original. The camera cannot lie. Or, to be more accurate, it can lie; but the process of making it lie is tedious and expensive. The photographers had no sufficient inducement to improve my appearance. But the speech which accompanied the pictures and which was attributed to me, was beautifully unrecognizable. Such a paean in praise of capitalism and Mr Baldwin! It did one's heart good to read it. Labourism and Fabian prejudices are not popular in America. The reporters had made me respectable. It was meant, no doubt, as an act of kindness. Still I should have preferred it if they had emended my face rather than my opinions.

On the Train

The Daylight Limited takes just twelve hours to run from Frisco to Los Angeles. And through what various landscapes!

First the English home counties – a land like a park, checkered with small ploughed fields and swelling into little hills. The little hills became rolling downs, the downs grew larger and larger, until they were great mountains with mile-high slopes of grass and here and there a wood of dark evergreen trees. The mountains subsided, the land became drier and more barren, the grass disappeared. For an hour or two we were in a desert – miles upon miles of dust, fledged sparsely with the grey-leaved growth of a parched land. We might have been in Rajputana. But there, suddenly, on the right, was the Pacific, for ever breaking and breaking on its desolate beaches.

'One hundred and thirteen miles along the shores of the Ocean,' a gentleman in uniform obligingly informed us, and then tried to sell us tinted spectacles that we might comtemplate the Ocean without discomfort. 'Sci-en-tifically made to exclude the ultra-violet rays. The price is one dollar only.' All day, at intervals of half an hour, he walked up and down the train, telling us about the beauties and the wealth of California, and peddling, now postcards, now candies, now Californian figs and oranges, now chewing-gum and True Story Magazines. He was the only distraction on the train. In a desperation of *désoeuvrement* the passengers bought whatever he offered.

'One hundred and thirteen miles along the shores of the Ocean.' Before we had passed the hundred and thirteenth milestone, the country had changed again – had changed from the sea-coast of Rajputana to that of Italy. The deserts began to flourish. Groves of lemons and oranges flanked the railway. There were vineyards, and fields of corn, and bright flowers. Parallel with the sea, a range of elegant and florid mountains mimicked the Apuan Alps. A little architecture, and the illusion would have been complete. But there were no churches, no huge pink villas among the cypresses, no castles on the hills. Nothing but wooden shanties and little brick dog-kennels, dust heaps and oil-tanks and telegraph poles, and the innumerable motor-cars of the most prosperous country in the world.

Los Angeles. A Rhapsody

First Movement

Daylight had come to the common folk of Hollywood, the bright Californian daylight. But within the movie studio there shone no sun, only the lamps, whose intense and greenish-yellow radiance gives to living men and women the appearance of jaundiced corpses. In a corner of one huge barn-like structure they were preparing to 'shoot.' The camera stood ready, the corpse-lights were in full glare. Two or three cowboys and a couple of clowns lounged about, smoking. A man in evening dress was trusting to his moustache to make him look like an English villain. A young lady, so elegant, so perfectly and flawlessly good-looking that you knew her at once for the Star, was sitting in a corner, reading a book. The Director – it seemed a waste that such a profile should be *au-dessus de la mêlée* instead of in the pictures – gave her a courteous hail. Miss X looked up from her literature. 'It's the scene where you see the murder being committed,' he explained. Miss X got up, put away the book and beckoned to her maid, who brought her a comb and a mirror. 'My nose all right?' she asked, dabbing on powder. 'Music!' shouted the Director. 'Make it emotional.' The band, whose duty it is in every studio to play the actors into an appropriate state of soul, struck up a waltz. The studio was filled with a sea of melodic treacle; our spirits rocked and wallowed on its sticky undulations. Miss X handed back her powder-puff to the maid and walked up to the camera. 'You hide behind that curtain and look out,' the Director explained. Miss X retired behind the curtain. 'Just the hand first of all,' the Director went on. 'Clutching. Then the face, gradually.' 'Yes, Mr Z,' came the quiet voice of the Star from behind the hanging plush. 'Ready?' asked the Director. 'Then go ahead.' The camera began to purr, like a genteel variety of dentist's drill. The curtain slightly heaved. A white hand clutched at its edge. 'Terror, Miss X,' called the Director. The white hand tightened its clutch in a spasm of cinematographic fear. The Director nodded to the bandmaster. 'Put some pep into it,' he adjured. Pep was put in; the billows of treacle rose higher. 'Now the face, Miss X. Slowly. Just one eye. That's good. Hold it. A little more terror.' Miss X heart-rendingly registered her alarm. 'That's good. That's very good. O.K.' The camera stopped purring. Miss X came out from behind the curtain and walked back to her chair. Reopening her book, she went on quietly reading about Theosophy.

We moved on and, after halting for a few moments on our way to watch some more terror being registered (by a man this time and under a different Director), penetrated into the secret places of the studio. We pronounced passwords, quoted the Manager's permission, disclaimed connections with rival companies, and were finally admitted. In one room they were concocting miracles and natural cataclysms – typhoons in bathtubs and miniature earthquakes, the Deluge, the Dividing of the Red Sea, the Great War in terms of toy tanks and Chinese fire-crackers, ghosts and the Next World. In another they were modelling prehistoric animals and the architecture of the remote future. In cellars below ground, mysteriously lighted by red lamps and smelling of chemicals, a series of machines was engaged in developing and printing the films. Their output was enormous. I forget how many thousands of feet of art and culture they could turn out each day. Quite a number of miles, in any case.

Second Movement

Emerging, I bought a newspaper. It was Saturday's; a whole page was filled with the announcements of rival religious sects, advertising the spiritual wares that they would give away or sell on the Sabbath. 'Dr Leon Tucker with the Musical Messengers in a Great Bible Conference. 3 Meetings To-morrow. Organ Chimes, Giant Marimbaphone, Vibraphone, Violin, Piano, Accordion, Banjo, Guitar and other Instruments. Wilshire Baptist Church.' The Giant Marimbaphone was certainly tempting. But in the First Methodist Church (Figueroa at Twentieth) they were going to distribute 'Mother's Day Flowers for Worshippers.' (On Mother's Day you must wear a red carnation if your mother is alive, a white one if she is dead. The florists are everywhere the most ardent of matriolaters.) Moreover, they had booked the exclusive services of Dr James H. Maclaren, Dramatic Orator, who was going to give his well-known stunt, 'Impersonations of Lincoln and Roosevelt.' 'Dr Maclaren,' we were informed, 'comes with a unique, original, eloquent, instructive and inspiring Message concerning two of our Great Presidents. Uplifting and inspiring. It will do your soul good. The wonderful Messages of these two Great Presidents will be brought home with new emphasis and you will feel that you have spent the evening in the company of Great Spirits. Hear the great organ, Quartet of Artists and Vested Chorus.' At the Hollywood Congregational Church there were to be moving pictures of Jackie Coogan in his crusade to the Near East; the prospect was a draw. But then so was the photograph of Miss Leila Castberg of the Church of Divine Power (Advanced Thought); her performance might not be very interesting – she was scheduled to preach at the Morosco Theater on Divine Motherhood – but the face which looked out from her advertisement was decidedly pleasing. Less attractive, to the devout male at any rate, were the photos of Messrs Clarke and Van Bruch; but the phrasing of their ad. was enought to counteract in the mind of the reader the effect produced by their portraits. 'IT'S ON, FOLKS, IT'S ON,' so the announcement ran. 'The tide is rising at an OLD-FASHIONED REVIVAL. Every night except Monday. 7.30 P.M. Soul-stirring sermons and songs. Special to-night! Hear 10 Evangelists – 10. Van Bruch–Clarke Evangelistic Party.'

Jazz it up, jazz it up. Keep moving. Step on the gas. Say it with dancing. The Charleston, the Baptists, Radios and Revivals. Uplift and Gilda Gray. The pipe organ, the nigger with the saxophone, the Giant Marimbaphone. Hymns and the movies and Irving Berlin. Petting Parties and the First Free United Episcopal Methodist Church. Jazz it up! 'N. C. Beskin, the CONVERTED JEW, back from a successful tour, will conduct a tabernacle campaign in Glendale. 'WHY I BECAME A CHRISTIAN?' Dressed in Jewish garb. Will exhibit interesting paraphernalia.' Positively the last appearance. The celebrated Farmyard Imitations. 10 Evangelists – 10. The finest troupe of Serio-Comic Cyclists ever. Onward Christian Soldiers. Abide with me. I'm gonna bring a water melon to my girl to-night.

THIRD MOVEMENT

Mother's Day. (Mr Herring of Indiana, 'The Father of Mother's Day.') But why not Flapper's Day? It would be more representative, more democratic, so to speak. For in Joy City there are many more Flappers – married as well as unmarried – than Mothers.

> Nunc vitiat uterum quae vult formosa videri,
> Raraque in hoc aevo est quae velit esse parens.

Thousands and thousands of flappers, and almost all incredibly pretty. Plumply ravishing, they give, as T. S. Eliot has phrased it, a 'promise of pneumatic bliss.' Of pneumatic bliss, but of not much else, to judge by their faces. So curiously uniform, unindividual and blank. Hardly more expressive – to the foreign eye, at any rate – than any of the other parts of that well-contoured anatomy which they are at such pains to display.

On the beaches of the Pacific that display was indeed superb. Mack Sennett Bathing Beauties by the hundred. They gambolled all around us, as we walked up and down in the windy sunlight along

the sands. Frisking temptations. But we were three St Anthonies –
Charlie Chaplin and Robert Nichols and I – three grave theologians
of art, too deeply absorbed in discussing the way of cinematographic
salvation to be able to bestow more than the most casual attention
on the Sirens, however plumply deserving.

FOURTH MOVEMENT

Cocktail time. (We've dealt with the same bootlegger for upwards of
two years now. A most reliable man.) Ice rattles in the shaker – a
dance of miniature skeletons – and the genuinely reliable liquor is
poured out. *À boire, à boire!* Long live Pantagruel! This is dry
America. We climbed into our host's car and drove, it seemed
interminably, through the immense and sprawling city. Past movie
palaces and theatres and dance halls. Past shining shops and
apartments and enormous hotels. On every building the vertical
lines of light went up like rockets into the dark sky. And the
buildings themselves – they too had almost rocketed into existence.
Thirty years ago Los Angeles was a one-horse – a half-horse – town.
In 1940 or thereabouts it is scheduled to be as big as Paris. As big
and as gay. The great Joy City of the West.

And what joy! The joy of rushing about, of always being busy, of
having no time to think, of being too rich to doubt. The joy of
shouting and bantering, of dancing and for ever dancing to the noise
of the savage music, of lustily singing.

> (Yes, sir, she's my Baby.
> No, sir, don't say 'Maybe.'
> Yes, sir, she's my Baby now.)

The joy of loudly laughing and talking at the top of the voice about
nothing. (For thought is barred in this City of Dreadful Joy and
conversation is unknown.) The joy of drinking prohibited whiskey
from enormous silver flasks, the joy of cuddling provocatively bold
and pretty flappers, the joy of painting the cheeks, of rolling the eye
and showing off the desirable calves and figure. The joy of going to
the movies and the theatre, of sitting with one's fellows in luxurious
and unexclusive clubs, of trooping out on summer evenings with fifty
thousand others to listen to concerts in the open air, of being always
in a crowd, never alone. The joy of going on Sundays to hear a

peppy sermon, of melting at the hymns, of repenting one's sins, of getting a kick out of uplift. The joy, in a word, of having what is technically known as a Good Time.

And oh, how strenuously, how whole-heartedly the people of Joy City devote themselves to having a Good Time! The Good Times of Rome and Babylon, of Byzantium and Alexandria were dull and dim and miserably restricted in comparison with the superlatively Good Time of modern California. The ancient world was relatively poor; and it had known catastrophe. The wealth of Joy City is unprecedentedly enormous. Its lighthearted people are unaware of war or pestilence or famine or revolution, have never in their safe and still half-empty Eldorado known anything but prosperous peace, contentment, universal acceptance. The truest patriots, it may be, are those who pray for a national calamity.

On and on we drove, through the swarming streets of Joy City. (One automobile, sir, to every three and a quarter inhabitants.) The tall buildings impended, the lights whizzed up like rockets. On and on. Across an open space there suddenly loomed up a large white building, magically shining against the intensified blackness of the sky behind. (Just finished, sir, the Temple of the Elks.) From its summit the beams of half a dozen searchlights waved to heaven. They seemed the antennae of some vast animal, feeling and probing in the void – for what? For Truth, perhaps? Truth is not wanted in the City of Dreadful Joy. For Happiness? It is possessed. For God? But God had already been found; he was inside the shining Temple; he *was* the Temple, the brand new, million-dollar Temple, in which at this moment the initiates of the venerable Order of Elks were congregated to worship, not the effetely aristocratic Lady Poverty, but plain American Mrs Wealth. Five or six hundred motor-cars stood parked outside the doors. What *could* those luminous antennae be probing for? Why, for nothing, of course, for nothing! If they waved so insistently, that was just for fun. Waving for waving's sake. Movement is a joy, and this is the Great Joy City of the West.

Fifth Movement

The restaurant is immense. The waiters sprint about, carrying huge dishes of the richest food. What Gargantuan profusion! Great ten-pound chops, square feet of steak, fillets of whale, whole turkeys stewed in cream, mountains of butter. And the barbarous music throbs and caterwauls unceasingly. Between each juicy and satiating course, the flappers and the young men dance, clasped in an amorous wrestle. How Rabelais would have adored it! For a week, at any rate. After that, I am afraid, he would have begun to miss the conversation and the learning, which serve in his Abbey of Thelema as the accompaniment and justification of pleasure. This Western pleasure, meaty and raw, untempered by any mental sauce – would even Rabelais' unsqueamish stomach have been strong enough to digest it? I doubt it. In the City of Dreadful Joy Pantagruel would soon have died of fatigue and boredom. *Taedium laudamus* – so reads (at any rate for the inhabitants of Rabelais' continent) the triumphant canticle of Californian joy.

The restaurant is suddenly plunged into darkness. A great beam of light, like the Eye of God in an old engraving, stares down from somewhere near the ceiling, right across the room, squinting this way and that, searching – and at last finding what it had been looking for: a radiant figure in white, the singer of the evening. A good, though not superlatively good singer in the style of Ethel Levey or Jenny Golder.

> You gotta feed a chicken corn,
> You gotta feed a seal fish,
> You gotta feed a man (significant pause and *œillade)* Love.

And so on. The enthusiasm which greets these rhymed lectures in elementary physiology is inordinate. Being enthusiastic is a joy. We are in Joy's metropolis.

There is a final burst of applause. The divine eyelid closes down over God's shining eye. The band strikes up again. The dancing rebegins. The Charleston, the fox-trot. 'There is only one first-class civilization in the world to-day. It is right here, in the United States and the Dominion of Canada.' Monkeyville, Bryan, the Ku Klux Klan. 'Europe's is hardly second class, and Asia's is fourth to sixth class.' Jazz it up; jazz it up! And what did late, great Ambassador Page have to say? 'The whole continent (of Europe) is rotten, or tyrannical, or yellow dog. I wouldn't give Long Island or Moore County for the whole continent of Europe.' And with Coney Island added to Long Island and Los Angeles in the scale along with Moore County, he might have thrown in all Asia and the British

Empire. Three cheers for Page! Yes, sir, 'American idealism has made itself felt as a great contributory force to the advancement of mankind.' Three cheers for George F. Babbitt and the Rotary Club! And three cheers for Professor Nixon Carver! 'Prosperity,' the Professor has said, 'is coming to us precisely because our ideas are not materialistic. All these things (e.g. the Elks' Temple, the jazz bands, the movie palaces, the muffins at breakfast) are added to us precisely because we are seeking the Kingdom of God and His righteousness.' Three cheers more – thrice three! The Prof. deserves them.

It is almost midnight. A few minutes and it will be the Sabbath. A few hours and the Giant Marimbaphone will be proclaiming the glory of the new billion-dollar God. At the Ambassador Hotel (alas, too expensive for me to stay at) Dr Ernest Holmes will be preaching on 'The Science of Jesus.' It is time to go home. Farewell, farewell. Parting is such sweet sorrow. Did Tosti raise his bowler hat when he said 'Good-bye'?

Chicago

Turning over the pages of the Chicago telephone directory, I came upon a full-page advertisement of a firm of undertakers, or 'morticians,' as they are now more elegantly styled in America. The type was large and bold; my eye was fatally caught. I interrupted my search to read, in twenty lines of lyrical prose, an appreciation of the incomparable Service which Kalbsfleisch and Company were rendering to Society. Their shop, I learned, was a mortuary chapel in the Gothic style; their caskets (the grosser English would call them coffins) were elegant, silk-lined and cheap; their motor-hearses were funereally sumptuous; their manners towards the bereaved were grave, yet cheering, yet purposefully uplifting; and they were fortunate in being able to 'lay the Loved Ones to rest in —— Graveyard, the Cemetery Unusual.' Service was their motto and always would be. Service whole-hearted and unflagging. And to prove that they meant it, personally and individually, they had reproduced two photographs, one of Mr Kalbsfleisch, the Governing Director of the Firm, and the other of charming Mrs Kalbsfleisch, Licensed Embalmer.

I remained for some time in meditative contemplation of Mrs

Kalbsfleisch's smile; I re-read more than once her husband's poetical and uplifting prose. The page on which I now gazed was something more, I reflected, than a mere page of advertising in a telephone book. It was a page out of contemporary American history. Something is happening on the western shore of the Atlantic, something that has already made America unlike any other country in the world, something that threatens to separate it still further from the older civilizations, unless (which God forbid) the older civilizations should themselves fall victims to the same distorting process. To any one who reads and inwardly digests Mr Kalbsfleisch's advertisment in the Chicago telephone book, the nature of this strange historical process becomes clear. The page is a symptom and a revealing symbol.

The thing which is happening in America is a revaluation of values, a radical alteration (for the worse) of established standards. Mr Kalbsfleisch shows us how far the process has already gone. How much further it may go we cannot guess, nor to what consummation it will lead, nor whether there may be reactions and counter-processes.

There are two ways in which the existing standards of values may be altered. In the first case, the very existence of values may be denied. In the second, values are admitted, but the mode in which they are assigned is changed: things which in the past had been regarded as possessing great value are disparaged, or, more often, things which were previously considered of small value come to be regarded as precious.

In Europe such attempts as have been made to alter the existing standards of values have generally taken the form of denials of the existence of values. Our belief that things possess value is due to an immediate sense or intuition; we feel, and feeling we know, that things have value. If men have doubted the real existence of values, that is because they have not trusted their own immediate and intuitive conviction. They have required an intellectual, a logical and 'scientific' proof of their existence. Now such a proof is not easily found at the best of times. But when you start your argumentation from the premises laid down by scientific materialism, it simply cannot be discovered. Indeed, any argument starting from these premises must infallibly end in a denial of the real existence of values. Fortunately human beings are capable of enormous inconsistencies, and the eighteenth- and nineteenth- century men of science, whose conception of the universe was such that values could not be regarded by them as possessing any sort of real existence, were in practice the most ardent upholders of the established standards of values.

Still, the materialist conception of the universe could not fail to exert an influence. The generation of Arnold and of Tennyson sat uncomfortably on the horns of what seemed an inescapable dilemma. Either the materialist hypothesis was true; in which case there was no such thing as value. Or else it was false; in which case values really existed, but science could not. But science manifestly *did* exist. The electric telegraph and the steam engine were there to prove it. The fact that you could go into any post office and communicate almost instantaneously with the antipodes was felt to be a confirmation of the materialistic hypothesis then current among men of science. It worked, therefore it was true, and therefore our intimate sense of the existence of values was a mere illusion. Tennyson and Arnold did not want it to be an illusion; they were distressed, they were inwardly divided. Their intellects denied what their feelings asserted; and the Truth (or rather what was at that time apparently the Truth) was at war with their hopes, their intuitive convictions, their desires. The European intellectuals of a later generation accepted the conclusions logically derivable from the scientific-materialist hypothesis and resigned themselves – almost with glee – to living in a devaluated world. Some of them are still with us, and the theories which they propounded, as corollaries to the main value-denying theory from which they started, are still influential. Claiming to speak as the apostles of scientific truth, they stripped art of its significance, they reinterpreted human life in terms, not of its highest, spiritual aspects, but of its lowest. (I am using the terms 'highest' and 'lowest,' which they, of course, would repudiate as nonsensical.) A less sophisticated generation had regarded the Sistine frescoes as being somehow superior to a prettily patterned rug, *Macbeth* as more important than *The Rape of the Lock*. Illusion! According to the apostles of scientific truth, one was really just as good as the other. Indeed, the *Rape* and the patterned rug were actually superior to *Macbeth* and the Michelangelo frescoes, as being more finished and perfect works of art: they aroused, it was explained, intenser 'aesthetic emotions.' Art thus satisfactorily disposed of, religion was next 'explained' in terms of sex. The moral conscience was abolished (another illusion) and 'amuse yourself' proclaimed as the sole categorical imperative. The theories of Freud were received in intellectual circles with acclaim; to explain every higher activity of the human mind in terms of incest and coprophily came to be regarded not only as truly scientific, but also as somehow virile and courageous. Freudism became the *realpolitik* of psychology and philosophy. Those who denied values felt themselves to be rather heroic; instinctively they were appealing to the standards which they were trying, intellectually, to destroy.

Meanwhile the men of science are finding that the crude materialism of their predecessors is a hypothesis that will not work. Our apostles of scientific truth find themselves the apostles of what will soon be universally regarded as a fallacy.

But the influence of these *ci-devant* 'scientific' deniers of values has not been wide. In most human beings the intuitive sense of values is too strong to be seriously affected by intellectual arguments, however specious. They are revolted by the denial of values; they insist on interpreting the world in terms of high and low. Unfortunately, however, they are apt to make mistakes and to call things by the wrong names, labelling 'high' what should rightly be low, and 'low' what ought to be high. This falsification of the standard of values is a product, in our modern world, of democracy, and has gone furthest in America. It is much more dangerous than the mere denial of values, because it is much more popular. To most men and women the denial of values is horrible; but the falsification of them so as to square with democratic prejudices is pleasant and flattering. Let us examine Mr Kalbsfleisch's advertisement to try to discover the direction in which standards have been perverted and the methods of falsification employed.

The democratic hypothesis in its extreme and most popular form is that all men are equal and that I am just as good as you are. It is so manifestly untrue that a most elaborate system of humbug has had to be invented in order to render it credible to any normally sane human being. Nowhere has this system of humbug been brought to such perfection as in America. Take the case of Mr Kalbsfleisch. He is an undertaker. The trade he practises has never enjoyed great esteem; for, although it is a necessary trade, it cannot be said to call for high intellectual or moral qualities in its practitioners. Mr Kalbsfleisch and his fellows have realized and resented this failure on the part of humanity to esteem them. Being good democrats, they want to insist on their equality with the admittedly best people. They begin by altering the name of their trade. The word 'undertaker' has base associations. They therefore coin a new locution and style themselves 'morticians.' 'Mortician' is a word that rhymes with such highly reputable words as physician, mathematician, academician, politician – not to mention Titian. What's in a name? Much. From having been undertakers and mere tradesmen, the morticians have become artists and members of an almost learned profession.

Having emended their name, the morticians proceed to exalt and magnify their calling. They do this in a very simple, but eminently effective way: by insisting on the Service which they render to Humanity.

The notion of Service is fundamental to Christianity. Jesus and his greatest followers have proclaimed the spiritual importance of Service and have exhorted all men and women to be the servants of their fellows. The morticians, and with them all the Business Men of America, are as whole-heartedly enthusiastic about Service as was ever St Francis or his divine Master. But the activities which they designate by the word 'Service' happen to be slightly different from those which the Founder of Christianity called by the same name. For Jesus and St Francis, Service connoted self-sacrifice, abnegation, humility. For the morticians and other American Business Men, Service means something else; it means doing profitable business efficiently and with just sufficient honesty to keep out of gaol. Ameri can Business Men talk like St Francis; but their activities are indistinguishable from those of the money-changers and the sellers of doves whom Jesus expelled from the Temple with a whip of small cords.

The money-changers and the bird-hawkers protested, no doubt, that they were serving humanity as well as, and even better than, their aggressor. 'What we do,' they must have argued, 'is useful and necessary; society finds us indispensable.' It is on the same ground – that they perform necessary jobs well – that American Business Men claim to be doing Service, and Service of the highest value. They overlook the significant historical fact that all the valuable things in life, all the things that make for civilization and progress, are precisely the unnecessary ones. All scientific research, all art, all religion are (by comparison with making coffins or breakfast foods) unnecessary. But if we had stuck to the merely necessary, we should still be apes. According to any proper standard of values, the unnecessary things and the unnecessary people who are concerned with them are much more important than the necessary ones. By exalting the merely necessary to an equality with the unnecessary, the American Business Man has falsified the standard of values. The Service rendered by a mortician or a realtor has come to be regarded as the equivalent of the Service rendered by an artist or a man of science. Babbitt can now honestly believe that he and his kind are doing as much for humanity as the Pasteurs and the Isaac Newtons. Kalbsfleisch among his silk-lined caskets knows himself to be as good as Beethoven. Successful stockbrokers, certain that Business is Religion, can come home after a day of speculation on the Exchange, feeling as virtuously happy as Buddha must have felt when he had renounced the world and received his great illumination.

In every part of the world and at all times the vast majority of human beings has consisted of Babbitts and peasants. They are indispensable; the necessary work must be done. But never, except at the present time, and nowhere but in America, have the necessary millions believed themselves the equals of the unnecessary few. In Europe the ancient standards still persist, the ghost at least of the old hierarchy survives. The rich parvenu may despise the man of science for his poverty; but he still feels humble before his knowledge, his superior intelligence and his disinterestedness. That technique of humbug, by the employment of which successful stockbroking may be made to seem as valuable and noble an occupation as scientific research or artistic creation, has not yet been perfected in Europe, it has hardly been invented. True, there are many people who would like to see the technique introduced, ready-made and perfected, from across the Atlantic. I trust, and I am even moderately confident, that they will be for ever disappointed.

Meanwhile, on the western side of the Atlantic the progressive falsification of values steadily continues. So far, what has happened is this: preciousness has been attributed to things and people previously regarded as possessing small value. But in certain parts of the Union the innumerable necessary men are preparing to move a step further. Not content with attributing the highest possible value to themselves, they are denying it to the unnecessary few; the majority has sovereign rights. What was previously held to be high is now being disparaged. The mental and moral qualities, the occupations and diversions of the greatest number are regarded as the best, the sole permissible; the qualities and occupations of the few are condemned. Stupidity, suggestibility and business are held up as supremely precious. Intelligence, independence and disinterested activity – once admired – are in process of becoming evil things which ought to be destroyed. In Tennessee and other remote provinces the crusade against them has already begun. It remains to be seen whether this further perversion of values will affect the rest of the continent.

New York

Now that liberty is out of date, equality an exploded notion and fraternity a proven impossibility, republics should change their mottoes. Intelligence, Sterility, Insolvency: that would do for contemporary France. But not for America. The American slogan would have to be something quite different. The national motto should fit the national facts. What I should write under America's flapping eagle would be: Vitality, Prosperity, Modernity.

Let us begin with the last, modernity. Modernity in this context may be defined as the freedom (at any rate in the sphere of practical, material life) from customary bonds and ancient prejudices, from traditional and vested interest; the freedom, in a word, from history. Change is accepted in America as the first and fundamental fact – and accepted, not as other peoples have accepted it, as an evil to be combated by the organization of a stable society, by the making of things too strong and solid for time to be able quickly to devour, but as a good, as the foundation and key of practical life. Most things in this modern land are provisional, made to last only till something better, or at any rate something newer, shall appear to take their place. All through the country the houses have an air of impermanence; the landscape, wherever the hand of man has touched it, looks sketchy and unfinished. The factories are perpetually renewing themselves; half their profits are ear-marked for the expenses of this chronic rejuvenation. Forty-year-old locomotives, having the strange and almost fabulous aspect of Tertiary monsters, still rumble over European rails. A respectable American railway company would think itself disgraced by the possession of an engine that was more than ten years of age. Nor would the engines survive much longer; things, here, are built to be scrapped as soon as they have outworn their first youth. Change is made much of, it is rejoiced in. That is modernity.

And then there is prosperity. America is a half-populated country teeming with natural wealth. Business methods are unhampered, except perhaps in the East, by the old traditions belonging to a vanished form of society. The traditions of an age of feudalism, of agriculture and of craftsmanship have done much to cramp the efficient and rational development of industrialism in Europe. The greater part of America started with a clean slate. In California there is one motor-car to every three inhabitants. Considering the Californian circumstances, it is not to be wondered at.

American vitality is a function, mathematically speaking, of the prosperity and the modernity. An insufficiently nourished human being requires a great deal of rest. Reduced to an Indian diet, Americans would be a good deal less interested than they actually are in business efficiency, uplift and the Charleston. They would spend most of their spare time in doze, or in the doze's first cousin: meditation. But they have enough to eat – a great deal more than enough, in fact. They can afford to hustle; indeed they must hustle or else die of a plethora. Men and women who wash down beefsteaks with glasses of rich creamy milk need to do something pretty strenuous in order to keep alive at all.

The psychological effects of prosperity are hardly less striking than the physical. In less fortunate countries the precariousness of existence keeps large classes of the population in a state of chronic fear. Unemployment is a haunting apprehension, both to manual workers and to those who wear black coats. So little is needed in Europe to precipitate the man of the middle class into the abysses of lower-classdom; the bottomless pit of poverty, into which so many of the manual workers have already fallen, gapes before his feet. Fear haunts and for ever darkly impends. Fear is the enemy of life; it inhibits every function of the mind and body. That is why, in the less fortunate parts of Europe, vitality is so low.

In America this fear hardly exists; there is no reason why any one should fail to earn good wages. Nor is the fall from the status of the clerk to that, shall we say, of the factory hand discreditable, as it would be in the older countries, where the prejudice against manual labour as something fundamentally degrading and unrespectable still lingers. The middle classes are therefore largely relieved of their terror of losing caste. Liberated from fear, the Americans live with confidence, and therefore with enhanced vitality. A generous extravagance, undreamed of in other parts of the world, is the American rule. Men and women earn largely and spend what they have on the national pleasures, which are all social and stimulative of vitality.

Modernity also tends to heighten vitality – or to be more exact, it affects the expression of vitality, externalizing it in the form of vehement action. The joyful acceptance of change, which so profoundly influences American industry, business methods and domestic architecture, reacts on the affairs of daily, personal life. Pleasure is associated with a change of place and environment, finally with mere movement for its own sake. People leave their homes if they want entertainment. They externalize their vitality in visiting places of public amusement, in dancing and motoring – in doing anything that is not quietly sitting by their own fireside (or rather by their own radiator). What is known as 'night life' flourishes in America as nowhere else in the world. And nowhere, perhaps, is there so little conversation. In America vitality is given its most obviously vital expression. Hence there appears to be even more vitality in the Americans than perhaps there really is. A man may have plenty of vitality and yet keep still; his motionless calm may be mistaken for listlessness. There can be no mistake about people who dance and rush about. American vitality is always obviously manifested. It expresses itself vigorously to the music of the drum and saxophone, to the ringing of telephone bells and the roar of street cars. It expresses itself in terms of hastening automobiles, of huge and yelling crowds, of speeches, banquets, 'drives,' slogans, sky signs. It is all movement and noise, like the water gurgling out of a bath – down the waste. Yes, down the waste.

New York

America is popularly supposed to be a country of Puritanism. And so it is, as any one who travels across it can discover. But what the traveller also discovers – to his vast surprise, if he happens to have arrived with conventional opinions about the country – is that a Rabelaisian looseness is just as characteristic of contemporary America as puritanical strictness. In Philadelphia the respectable booksellers do not stock Mr Cabell's *Jurgen*. In Boston the Watch and Ward Society suppresses the American *Mercury*, and in the same city one at least of my own novels has to be sold under the counter as though it were whiskey. I have been in Middle Western hotels where it was considered indecent for my wife to smoke a cigarette in the public rooms. And though I have not visited the Southern States, I have read in the newspapers the most extraordinary accounts of the persecutions to which unfaithful wives and errant husbands are liable there. It would be possible to quote many other examples of American puritanism. The list would be long and curious. These few specimens, however, are sufficient to prove the old contention that America is a puritanical country.

But it is also and simultaneously one of the least puritanical countries I have ever visited. In the theatres of New York it is possible to see plays of a character which can hardly be paralleled in any other city of the world. I do not speak of the displays of naked women; these have now become too commonplace to be remarked on – except, perhaps, in a country colonized by the Pilgrim Fathers. And in any case, Puritans tolerate spectacles and actions much more willingly than they tolerate words. It is only during the last few months that the Lord Chamberlain of England has finally brought himself to license the public performance of Bernard Shaw's play, *Mrs Warren's Profession*. Countless performances, whose appeal was frankly pornographic, have been licensed during the quarter-century of Mrs Warren's exile from the stage. Shaw's crime was to have discussed frankly and seriously the subject of prostitution. He broached certain ideas, used certain words. Puritans like to wear the fig-leaf over the mouth. This puritanical idiosyncrasy renders all the more remarkable the verbal frankness of many of the plays current in New York during the past months – plays in which there was no exposure of skin, but where spades were openly called spades, and often worse, more intimate names. I remember, for example, a play called *Cradle Snatchers*. It was a Restoration comedy brought up to date – Wycherley without the wit. Indeed, it was a little more than Restoration. Its theme, which concerns three middle-aged ladies, who hire three young men as lovers, is very close to that of a comedy of Fletcher's, *The Custom of the Country*, which Dryden, when defending the Restoration Theatre against the attacks of Jeremy Collier, pronounced to be far more indecent than any play written in his own day.

Nor was this play an isolated phenomenon. *Sex* lived up to its simple name. *Lulu Belle* and *The Shanghai Gesture* were no less remarkable. The fruitiest passage in *Gentlemen prefer Blondes*, which was playing when I passed through Chicago, had a robustly Rabelaisian humour, which I for one enormously enjoyed. But what did Mr Sumner of the New York Vice Society think of those Gargantuan jokes? What about chaste Mr Chase from Boston? And what would have been the reaction of those two lineal descendants of the Pilgrim Fathers to the casual, light-hearted references to homosexuality which I heard at more than one burlesque show and cabaret? I wonder.

It is not alone in the theatre that this spirit of anti-puritanism exhibits itself; it is also in American life. In one part of the country cigarette smoking will be forbidden, and the self-appointed censors of public morality will hold up passing automobiles and demand to see the marriage certificates of their occupants. In another the relations of the sexes will be easy, intimate and (how shall I phrase it?) chronically amorous. Fresh from the conventionalities and decorum of Paris and London, the stranger coming to the West Coast will be astonished by the amount of casual embracement, squeezing and public kissing which he sees going on, among the most respectable members of society, in restaurants and dancing-places. He will be astonished by the frankness with which people discuss their intimate affairs – in voices, moreover, so loud that the most private details are reverberatingly audible for yards around. He will be impressed by the almost Congolese style of dancing, while that general atmosphere of hilarious inebriation which pervades the night life of all American cities will make him wonder whether a little less Prohibition – which means a little less whiskey – might not perhaps be a good thing. In modern America the Rome of Cato and the Rome of Heliogabalus co-exist and flourish with an unprecedented vitality.

London

So the journey is over and I am back again where I started, richer by much experience and poorer by many exploded convictions, many perished certainties. For convictions and certainties are too often the concomitants of ignorance. Of knowledge and experience the fruit is generally doubt. It is a doubt that grows profounder as knowledge more deeply burrows into the underlying mystery, that spreads in exact proportion as experience is widened and the perceptions of the experiencing individual are refined. A fish's convictions, we may be sure, are unshakable. A dog is as full of certainty as the Veteran Liberal who has held the same opinions for forty years. You might implore a cat, as Cromwell by the bowels of Christ once implored a parliament, to bethink it that it might be mistaken; the beast would never doubt but that it was right.

I set out on my travels knowing, or thinking that I knew, how men should live, how be governed, how educated, what they should believe. I knew which was the best form of social organization and to what end societies had been created. I had my views on every activity of human life. Now, on my return, I find myself without any of these pleasing certainties. Before I started, you could have asked me almost any question about the human species and I should glibly have returned an answer. Ask a profoundly ignorant man how the electric light works; he finds the question absurdly simple. 'You just press the button,' he explains. The working electrician would give you a rather more technical account of the matter in terms of currents, resistances, conductivity. But the philosophical physicist would modestly confess his ignorance. Electrical phenomena, he would say, can be described and classified. But as for saying what electricity may be . . . And he would throw up his hands. The better you understand the significance of any question, the more difficult it becomes to answer it. Those who like to feel that they are always right and who attach a high importance to their own opinions should stay at home. When one is travelling, convictions are mislaid as easily as spectacles; but unlike spectacles, they are not easily replaced.

My own losses, as I have said, were numerous. But in compensation for what I lost, I acquired two inportant new convictions: that it takes all sorts to make a world, and that the established spiritual values are fundamentally correct and should be maintained. I call these opinions 'new,' though both are at least as old as civilization and though I was fully convinced of their truth before I started. But truths the most ancient, the most habitually believed, may be endowed for us as the result of new experience with an appearance of apocalyptic novelty. There is all the difference in the world between believing academically, with the intellect, and believing personally, imtimately, with the whole living self. A deaf man who had read a book about music might be convinced, theoretically, that Mozart was a good composer. But cure his deafness, take him to listen to the G minor Symphony; his conviction of Mozart's greatness would become something altogether new.

Of the fact that it takes all sorts to make a world I have been aware ever since I could read. But proverbs are always platitudes until you have personally experienced the truth of them. The newly arrested thief knows that honesty is the best policy with an intensity of conviction which the rest of us can never experience. And to realize that it takes all sorts to make a world one must have seen a certain number of the sorts with one's own eyes. Having seen them and having in this way acquired an intimate realization of the truth of the proverb, one finds it hard to go on complacently believing that one's own opinions, one's own way of life are alone rational and right. This conviction of man's diversity must find its moral expression in the practice of the completest possible tolerance.

But if travel brings a conviction of human diversity, it brings an equally strong conviction of human unity. It inculcates tolerance, but it also shows what are the limits of possible toleration. Religions and moral codes, forms of government and of society are almost endlessly varied, and each has a right to its separate existence. But a oneness underlies this diversity. All men, whatever their beliefs, their habits, their way of life, have a sense of values. And the values are everywhere and in all kinds of society broadly the same. Goodness, beauty, wisdom and knowledge, with the human possessors of these qualities, the human creators of things and thoughts endowed with them, have always and everywhere been honoured.

Our sense of values is intuitive. There is no proving the real existence of values in any way that will satisfy the logical intellect. Our standards can be demolished by argumentation; but we are none the less right to cling to them. Not blindly, of course, nor uncritically. Convinced by practical experience of man's diversity, the traveller will not be tempted to cling to his own inherited national standard, as though it were necessarily the only true and unperverted one. He will compare standards; he will search for what is common to all; he will observe the ways in which each standard is perverted, he will try to create a standard of his own that shall be as far as possible free from distortion. In one country, he will perceive, the true, fundamental standard is distorted by an excessive emphasizing of hierarchic and aristocratic principles; in another by an excess of democracy. Here, too much is made of work and energy for their own sakes; there, too much of mere being. In certain parts of the world he will find spirituality run wild; in others a stupid materialism that would deny the very existence of values. The traveller will observe these various distortions and will create for himself a standard that shall be, as far as possible, free from them – a standard of values that shall be as timeless, as uncontingent on circumstances, as nearly absolute as he can make them. Understanding diversity and allowing for it, he will tolerate, but not without limit. He will distinguish between harmless perversions and those which tend actually to deny or stultify the fundamental values. Towards the first he will be tolerant. There can be no compromise with the second.